HANDLING
EMERGENCIES

**Expect the Unexpected—Know What to Do
When You Need to Do It**

The Best Advice, Straight to the Point!

Reader's
digest

The Reader's Digest Association, Inc. New York, NY/Montreal

A READER'S DIGEST BOOK

Copyright © 2016 The Reader's Digest Association, Inc.

All rights reserved. Unauthorized reproduction, in any manner, is prohibited.

Reader's Digest is a registered trademark of The Reader's Digest Association, Inc.

Photographers: Ruth Jenkinson, Lizzie Orme

Picture credits: 18 Colin Bowling/Practical Pictures; 36 Image Source/Photolibrary; 120 Angela Hampton Picture Library/Alamy; 130 Banana Stock/Photolibrary; 182 Sebastian Kaulitzki/Alamy

Illustrator: Tom Connell

The Reader's Digest Quintessential Guide to Handling Emergencies contains material first published in *What to Do in an Emergency*.

Library of Congress Cataloging-in-Publication Data
Reader's digest quintessential guide to handling emergencies / by the Editors at Reader's Digest.
    pages cm. -- (Rd quintessential guides)
  Includes index.
  ISBN 978-1-62145-250-8 (spiral bound) -- ISBN 978-1-62145-251-5 (epub) 1. Home accidents--Prevention--Handbooks, manuals, etc. 2. First aid in illness and injury--Handbooks, manuals, etc. 3. Emergencies--Handbooks, manuals, etc. I. Reader's Digest Association
  TX150.R43 2015
                                363.13'72--dc23

We are committed to both the quality of our products and the service we provide to our customers. We value your comments, so please feel free to contact us.

        The Reader's Digest Association, Inc.
        Adult Trade Publishing
        44 South Broadway
        White Plains, NY 10601

For more Reader's Digest products and information, visit our website:

        www.rd.com (in the United States)
        www.readersdigest.ca (in Canada)

Printed in China

10 9 8 7 6 5 4 3 2 1

HOW TO USE THIS BOOK

The Reader's Digest Quintessential Guide to Handling Emergencies assumes that you may have to deal with a difficult and dangerous situation without professional help. The instructions should enable you to minimize injury and damage and get effective help and support as swiftly as possible.

This book has been designed to help you cope with a range of possible situations, some that all of us may face one day; others much rarer. The first three chapters deal with problems arising in your home, including general situations, fires, and water damage. The next chapter focuses on medical emergencies, including key life-saving techniques and critical signs. The final chapter concentrates on first aid.

Important: The information in this book has been carefully researched and all efforts have been made to ensure safety and accuracy. The Reader's Digest Association, Inc., does not assume any responsibility for any injuries suffered or losses incurred as a result of following the instructions in this book. Before taking any action based on information in this book, study the information carefully and make sure you understand it fully. Observe any warnings and "take care" notices.

WARNING

- **Medication:** Always follow the package instructions when taking medication and be aware of any contraindications. If you're unsure, consult a pharmacist or your GP for advice.

- **Emergency calls:** It is illegal to use a handheld phone while driving. You must try to pull over to a safe spot before making a phone call, even in an emergency.

CONTENTS

HOME SAFETY AND EMERGENCIES

MEDICAL EMERGENCIES AND FIRST AID

HOME
SAFETY
AND EMERGENCIES

GENERAL ISSUES

Solving problems in and around the house.

CARBON MONOXIDE BUILD-UP

Carbon monoxide (CO) is produced when gas is not properly burned in a faulty or poorly maintained gas appliance. It has no smell, so you cannot detect it, though you may show signs of a number of physical symptoms if exposed to the gas. If allowed to build up, it can lead to serious poisoning and, ultimately, death.

- You cannot see, taste, or smell carbon monoxide, but it can kill you without warning in a matter of hours.

- The physical symptoms of CO poisoning are tiredness, drowsiness, headaches, nausea, and pains in the chest and stomach, all of which can be confused with the symptoms of the flu or normal tiredness.

- An appliance may produce carbon monoxide if it is poorly installed or maintained, if there is a lack of fresh air for safe combustion of the gas, or if there is a blocked chimney.

- You are at particular risk if you sleep in a room with a gas appliance such as a gas fireplace or water heater, which is left on at night and does not have a fresh air intake. A fresh air intake allows the products of combustion of the gas to be taken outside and fresh air for combustion to be drawn in.

1. **Disperse gas.** Open all doors and windows to allow any gas to disperse.

2. **Vacate area.** Tell the rest of the family and move them out of harm's way. Notify your neighbors.

3. **Shut off gas supply.** If possible, turn off the faulty appliance or turn the gas off at the main gas tap. Phone your gas utility immediately.

4. **Suspect symptoms.** If you are suffering from physical symptoms only when at home, visit your doctor or local hospital and tell them you suspect carbon monoxide poisoning.

Carbon monoxide alarms

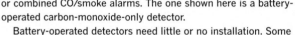

Carbon monoxide alarms warn of a leak. Since CO is colorless, tasteless, and odorless (unlike smoke from a fire), detection in a home environment is impossible without such a warning device. They can be hardwired or battery-operated, carbon monoxide only or combined CO/smoke alarms. The one shown here is a battery-operated carbon-monoxide-only detector.

Battery-operated detectors need little or no installation. Some hardwired detectors plug into an outlet, whereas others are wired into a circuit and need to be installed by an electrician. Refer to the manufacturer's instructions for the optimum location for any detector that you buy.

CHIMNEY COLLAPSES

 A chimney collapsing is—fortunately—a rare occurrence, but it can cause serious damage to your own and other properties and potentially to people passing nearby. There is nothing you can do if a natural disaster causes the collapse, but you can take steps to ensure that your chimney is not a danger.

- Chimneys can collapse in a serious storm. At least some of those that collapsed would have been weakened beforehand by other causes.

- A chimney fire can weaken chimney stacks because it causes the chimney to expand, which can crack the masonry.

- Cracking can also occur because of failed mortar pointing or failed chimney flashing, allowing water to get into the brickwork. If the water freezes, it expands, leading to cracking.

- A satellite dish (or large TV antenna) can cause structural damage to a chimney, especially if it is mounted on a long pole and exposed to strong winds.

- If the flue liner in a chimney is damaged or missing, combustion gases will destroy the mortar joints, causing the chimney to lean and eventually collapse. Make sure your chimney has a stainless steel liner or a cast-in-place cement liner.

1. **Get help.** Call emergency services. The fire department can help to make the property safe and an ambulance will be needed if anyone has been injured.

2. **Give first aid.** Do the best you can to help anyone who has been injured. If you are not sure what to do, ask the 911 dispatcher when you call them.

3. **Call a contractor.** What is left of the chimney will need to be secured and the roof weatherproofed to prevent further damage to your property and to any possessions.

4. **Contact insurance company.** Damage caused by a collapsed chimney should be covered by your homeowner's insurance policy—the only exception might be if you have caused the collapse yourself by illegally removing the chimney breasts.

SAFE CHIMNEYS

Inspect your chimney regularly (from the ground with binoculars) looking for cracks, leaning brickwork, loose or missing mortar, and damage to flashing (the shaped bits of lead around the chimney stack). If you see any problems, hire a contractor to make repairs at once.

DOORS AND WINDOWS BROKEN

If you think that your home has been robbed, take care if you suspect that the burglar might still be inside. Call the police.

If a door has been forced to gain entry, it will need to be secured until repaired or replaced. Call a carpenter, especially if you are not confident about making temporary repairs.

Both broken glass and splintered wood can cause injuries, so always wear thick gloves when handling them—plus eye protectors when removing glass from a windowpane.

DAMAGED DOOR

1. **Fix the damage.** If the door has been forced, it is likely that the door frame will have been damaged so that the lock is useless. Contact a carpenter or contractor to replace the frame, and the door, if necessary, so the door can be locked.

2. **Make temporary repairs.** An inward-opening front door with a letter box at about waist height and with a wooden floor on the inside can be temporarily secured with a strong piece of wood (see box, right). An alternative, if the door and frame are of solid wood, is to install a barrel bolt or two on the inside. This works if the door is inward or outward opening.

BROKEN WINDOW

1. **Smash out the broken glass from the window with a hammer.** Get a window repair service to do this or wear gloves and eye protectors and spread dust sheets on both sides of the window.

2. **To keep the weather out, tape a sheet of 6-mil plastic sheeting over a window.** If your window has a wooden frame, hold the plastic sheeting more securely with wooden battens (shown here). A wooden-framed window can be boarded up with plywood cut to size and screwed or nailed in place.

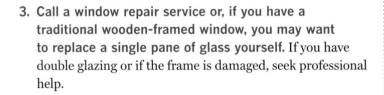

3. **Call a window repair service or, if you have a traditional wooden-framed window, you may want to replace a single pane of glass yourself.** If you have double glazing or if the frame is damaged, seek professional help.

Prop a door shut

1. **Cut the wood to length.** You will need around 4 feet of 2 x 4 lumber or similar for the prop and 1 foot for the floor support. This second piece of wood is screwed or nailed to the floor (watch for pipes or cables below).

2. **Secure the door.** With one end of the prop held in place by the floor support, jam the other end into the letter box. The prop can be kicked out if you need to open the door in a hurry.

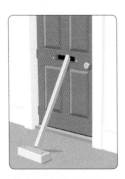

GAS LEAK

Natural gas leaking from an appliance in your home is rare but dangerous. If a person is trapped in a room with leaking gas, it can result in asphyxiation and, if a leak builds up, the accumulated gas can cause a fire or explosion if set alight.

You should be able to smell a gas leak, as fuel gas is given a very distinctive odor to enable quick detection. Although natural gas detectors are available for the home, they are only necessary if you have no sense of smell. A weak smell of gas could be caused by a pilot light going out on a stove, gas water heater or gas fire, or by a stove burner flame going out. This is the first thing to check. If the smell of gas gets stronger, or persists after you have done these checks, you should take action immediately before the gas has a chance to build up.

1. **Turn off the gas.** Individual gas appliances have their own gas shutoff; the main gas shutoff is a big lever on the gas pipe next to the gas meter, shown above, in the ON position. Move the lever through 90 degrees to the OFF position and cut the gas supply.

2. **Avoid sparks and put out flames.** Do not touch any electrical switches, as turning them on or off may create a spark and trigger an explosion. Immediately snuff lit candles, turn off gas burners, and douse natural flame fires. Lit cigarettes should be extinguished immediately with water.

3. **Disperse gas.** Open all doors and windows to allow any gas to disperse.

4. **Vacate area.** Keep everyone away from the affected areas, as the fumes could become overwhelming. Tell your nearest neighbors and ask them to pass on the warning.

5. **Call your gas utility or 911.** They will need to be told your location, name, and telephone number; how many people are present; how long the smell has been noticeable; and if it is coming from a crawlspace or basement. Be ready to provide details of any special circumstances or access information.

TAKE CARE

- Gas appliances should be checked every 12 months for leaks or other problems.

- If you live in an apartment building and become aware of a smell of gas, turn off the supply to your apartment immediately. Follow the other steps, alerting people in neighboring apartments, and call the gas company or 911 explaining your situation; follow their advice.

GUTTER OVERFLOW

When it rains heavily, water can spill in a splashing torrent out of the gutter, rather than into the downspouts. If left, faulty gutters can cause water problems, as well as being annoying for you and your neighbors. Grab an umbrella and go outside to find out where the water is coming from, then take appropriate action or get professional help.

Gushing gutter leaks are most often the result of blockages within the gutter. These are usually caused by leaves and birds' nests and also by moss washed off the roof. Similar blockages can happen in the downspouts leading to the drains.

A spilling gutter may not be blocked—it could be that it is sagging (so water runs the wrong way), usually caused by failure of one or more of the gutter brackets. The gutter may also be split or leaking at a joint and will need a new joint or some sealant.

BLOCKED GUTTER

Wait until the rain has stopped before using a ladder to work on gutters and only do so if you feel confident working at a height. The ladder must be properly secured and at the correct angle—one yard out for every four yards up the wall.

1. **Prepare your tools.** Go up the ladder armed with a bucket (plus a hook to secure it to the ladder) and a gutter scoop or garden trowel. Wear gloves.

2. **Clear debris.** Stuff a rag into the top of the downspout and then work along the gutter from there, scooping the debris out and putting it into the bucket.

3. **Flush out.** Ask a helper to pass up the garden hose to you. He can then be directed to turn the faucet on and off as required so that you can flush the gutter until it is clear. Work from the high end down toward the downspout.

BLOCKED DOWNSPOUT

1. **Start at the top.** Downspout blockages usually occur in the elbows at the top. If you can remove this, clean it out under a faucet. If not, poke a garden hose into it and flush it out.

2. **Clear pipe.** Use a rag tied securely to a stick to clear out the rest of the pipe, from above and below.

LEAKING GUTTER OR JOINT

1. **Fit new seal.** With plastic gutters, you should be able to buy a new seal (gasket) for the brackets where lengths of gutter meet. This is simply pressed into place with the gutter removed.

2. **Use gutter sealant.** On metal gutters (and plastic gutters where no replacement seal is available), you can stop leaks by applying black sticky gutter sealant using a caulk gun, or with self-adhesive gutter repair tape.

TREE FALLS ON HOUSE

Serious weather events are rare, but tree damage to homes does occasionally happen. To prevent it, maintain the trees on your property. The best time of year to have a tree pruned to make it safe is late autumn when the leaves have fallen; prune broad-leaved evergreens in May.

1. **Get out.** Use whatever route is safest to leave the property. This may or may not be the same as your fire-escape route (see page 35).

2. **Call emergency services.** The fire department will come and make the house safe.

3. **Contact insurers.** Get in touch with your insurance company as soon as possible—they will need to agree to cover expensive removal and emergency repair procedures.

4. **Secure your home.** You will need a roofing contractor or repairman to fix the roof and any other structural damage. The first priority will be to make it waterproof so that there is no additional damage to your property and possessions. A tree trimmer will be needed to cut up and remove the tree. If you are unable to live in the house immediately, ensure it is not a looting target. Secure doors and windows and put valuables in temporary storage.

BE AWARE

- You can cut branches off a neighbor's tree that overhang your property—but the wood and any fruit still legally belong to them, so you should offer them back.

- A tree that has fallen on a house may not be stable. Stay well away from it and keep children and pets away until it has been made safe.

- Storm damage to houses by trees (and the cost of removing the tree if it has fallen on the house) is covered by most homeowner's insurance policies.

- If your tree falls on your neighbors' property, they will need to make a claim on their homeowner's insurance policy.

- Although unlikely to cause a sudden emergency, tree roots can extend under a property, causing damage to the foundations. The first signs of this might be cracks in the plaster inside the house or cracks in the brickwork on the outside. You are entitled to cut back encroaching tree roots— but it would be wise to take professional advice before doing so. If a neighbor has complained to you that your tree roots are damaging his property and you have failed to take action, you could be held responsible for any damage.

CENTRAL HEATING FAILURE

Regular maintenance of your heating (and air-conditioning) system will make it less likely that there will be a sudden failure. If you do have a failure, check the 8 things listed here before you call for repairs. We show a gas-fired, forced air furnace, but many of the checks apply to electric systems and hot water boilers.

NO HEAT (OR AIR-CONDITIONING)

1. **Check the thermostat.** Make sure the switch is on Heat (or Cool in the summer).

2. **Check shutoff switches and breakers.** Check the switch by the side of the furnace (or near the furnace) and make sure the circuit breaker controlling it is flipped on.

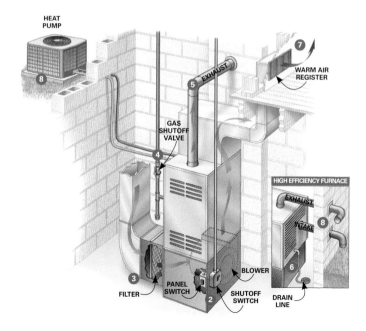

HEAT PUMP

EXHAUST

WARM AIR REGISTER

GAS SHUTOFF VALVE

HIGH EFFICIENCY FURNACE

EXHAUST

INTAKE

BLOWER

FILTER

PANEL SWITCH

SHUTOFF SWITCH

DRAIN LINE

3. **Change filters.** If the filter gets too clogged, the heat exchanger will shut off. If the filter looks dirty or the blower is running but no heat is coming out, replace the filter. It's located where the cold air return duct enters the furnace. Make sure the arrows on the filter face toward the furnace.

4. **Make sure the gas is on.** Someone may have turned the gas off. Look for a shutoff along the gas line feeding the furnace. If you have an older furnace, remove the front panel and make sure the pilot light is lit. If it won't stay lit, you probably need a new thermocouple.

5. **Mark sure the chimney exhaust is clear.** Birds sometimes find their way into the exhaust flue. Turn the furnace off and dismantle the duct.

6. **Flush out drain lines.** High-efficiency furnaces drain a lot of water, and if the drain line gets clogged, they'll shut down. Remove the drain hose and clean it with bleach and water (25% bleach). Let it soak for several minutes, then flush and reattach.

7. **Look for blocked or leaky ducts.** If one of your rooms is cold, make sure all the registers are open and not blocked by furniture. Also check the ductwork for gaps where warm air might be escaping.

8. **Clean debris from heat pumps and vents.** If your furnace vents out the side of the house, make sure nothing is blocking the intake or exhaust ducts. If ice is clogging one of the pipes, you have a bigger problem that needs a professional to fix. If you have a heat pump, clean off dirt and debris with a hose before heating season starts.

HOT WATER BOILER PROBLEMS
- **Thermocouple.** A thermocouple is a thick copper wire running from the gas control box outside the boiler to the

pilot light just inside the boiler. If the pilot light goes off, the thermocouple shuts off the gas. However, thermocouples sometimes wear out and must be replaced. Remove the cover and light the pilot, following the instructions on the cover of the boiler. If it won't stay lit, turn the gas and power off, remove the thermocouple, and buy an identical replacement at a hardware store.

- Circulating pump not working. Boilers have a circulating pump connected to the return water pipe near where it goes into the boiler. If the boiler is on but heat takes hours to reach the radiators, the pump may need repair or replacement—usually a job for the pros.

CLEAR A STEAM RADIATOR VENT
Don't confuse a hot water system with a steam system. Steam radiators have an air vent about halfway down the side. Unfortunately, many of these air vents get painted over, plugging the air hole, which prevents hot steam from coming into the radiator. Clear the air hole in the top of the vent with a small wire or sewing needle. Steam vents can also be replaced, but you'll have to go online or to a plumbing supply to find one.

Radiator problems
If your boiler and pump are working but some of the radiators are cool or cold, the problem could be in your radiators and pipes.

- **Cold tops and warm bottoms.** This is a sign that air has gotten into the system. Bleed the radiators with a radiator key to eliminate the air.

- **Cold radiators upstairs.** Bleed the radiators, as above. If this does not work, check the pump.

- **Cold bottoms and warm tops.** This indicates that you have corrosion and sludge is collecting at the bottom of the radiator. A plumber will flush out the sludge and add a corrosion inhibitor to the heating system.

NO HOT WATER

Life without hot water can be uncomfortable and the problem should be identified and solved as quickly as possible. There are some checks and repairs that you can do yourself, but for others you will need to get professional help.

GAS WATER HEATER

A water heater is basically a big holding tank. Beneath a gas water heater (shown here), a burner—similar to the one on a gas range—heats the tank.

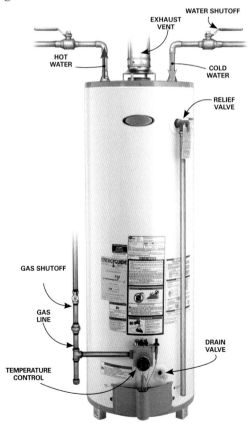

WATER SHUTOFF

EXHAUST VENT

HOT WATER

COLD WATER

RELIEF VALVE

GAS SHUTOFF

GAS LINE

TEMPERATURE CONTROL

DRAIN VALVE

REPLACE THE THERMOCOUPLE

The number 1 cause of pilot lights that won't stay lit is a worn-out thermocouple, but it's easy to replace.

1. **Remove the burner and thermocouple assembly.** Then detach the thermocouple from the burner and take it with you to the home center or hardware store to ensure you buy the right replacement.

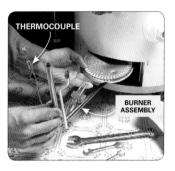

2. **Shut off the gas valve on the water heater and the gas valve on the gas line near the heater.** Then unfasten the three nuts that hold the thermocouple and the two gas tubes to the valve. The burner typically sits loosely—or under clips—in the burning chamber and just slides out. This is a good time to vacuum out the burner compartment, check for water leaks and remove debris in the burner ports. Attach the new thermocouple and reinstall the burner assembly. Light the pilot following the instructions on the water heater.

ELECTRIC WATER HEATER

Most residential electric water heaters have two heating elements: one near the top of the tank and one near the bottom. Power enters the top and runs to the high-temperature cutoff switch, and then to the thermostats and elements. The top and bottom elements are controlled by separate thermostats. When the water on the top of the tank is hot, the top element turns off and the lower one heats. The upper and lower heating elements never come on at the same time.

REPLACE ELECTRIC WATER HEATER ELEMENTS

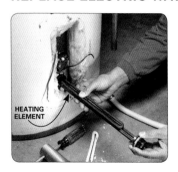

HEATING
ELEMENT

If your electric hot water heater has lukewarm or no hot water, there's a 90 percent chance that simply replacing the heating elements will solve the problem. The fix is straightforward, and replacement elements are inexpensive and readily available. Turn off the power to the water heater and the cold water supply to the heater, then drain the tank. Remove both access panels and disconnect the wires connected to the heating elements. Turn out the elements counterclockwise with a heating element wrench. Then install the new elements, reconnect the wires, fill the tank and turn the breaker on.

REPLACE A LEAKING WATER HEATER

Water heaters sometimes leak from the drain valve or relief valve. Those valves are easy to replace. But if a leak is coming from the tank it means the tank is starting to rust through and the hot water heater has to be replaced. If you have experience with plumbing, electrical and HVAC work—and have a helper available for heavy lifting—you can tackle the job yourself. Otherwise you'll have to call a plumber.

CAUTION!

Water heaters set too hot send thousands of people (mostly kids) to the emergency room each year. Most safety experts recommend a setting of 120°F. However, most temperature controls don't have numbers. To get an idea of how hot your water is, run hot water at the tap nearest the hot water heater for several minutes, then fill a glass and quickly put a cooking thermometer in it. If the reading is more than 120°, turn it down and check the temperature again at least 12 hours later.

NO ELECTRICITY

Your home's electrical system is a minor miracle. It takes one of the most dangerous forces in the universe and distributes it safely throughout your house, making everything you do easier and more convenient—except when the power goes off. Unless it's a utility company problem, there are measures you can take to get the power back on, but before you tackle the problem you should know a little about how the electrical system works (see box below on How Electricity is Supplied). Some things to keep in mind:

- The contents of a freezer will stay frozen (and so safe to eat) for several hours. To extend the period, cover it with blankets and do not open it.

- A power failure may cause a burglar alarm to go off. If you cannot reset it yourself, contact the alarm company and ask them to come and do it.

- If the power has failed and you are using candles for lighting, never leave them unattended. Be sure to keep children and pets away from naked flames.

How electricity is supplied

Electricity runs through underground or overhead power lines to an electrical meter, which measures your power use so the utility company can bill you. From there, it goes to your main circuit breaker panel, where the power is distributed to smaller wires running through your house. Some of these wires form general-purpose circuits that feed several lights and outlets; others create dedicated circuits which serve a single high-demand purpose, such as a fridge, electric baseboard heat, or kitchen countertop outlets.

NO POWER

Locate the tripped breaker. If the power for your whole house suddenly shuts off, it's almost always a utility company problem. All you can do is call the utility and alert them to the outage. However, if you lose power in just part of the house, it's means a breaker has tripped. Unplug or switch off everything that stopped working, then go to the circuit breaker box and look for a breaker in the halfway position. Push it all the way off, then flip it on.

Diagnose the cause. Breakers trip when the electrical circuit they control is overloaded or has a short circuit. If you've unplugged everything but the breaker still trips immediately after you reset it, there's a short circuit or some other problem somewhere. Leave the breaker off and call an electrician. However, if the breaker is working, chances are the circuit was just overloaded by too many devices drawing power at once—for instance, several electric heaters plugged into the same circuit. The breaker will also shut off it you plug in a defective device. Whatever the issue, do a little detective work until you isolate the cause.

GFCI OUTLETS

If none of the circuit breakers have tripped, the culprit is probably a GFCI ("ground fault circuit interrupter") outlet. GFCI outlets are required in damp or potentially damp areas of the house, where shock hazards are greatest. They protect against shocks by sensing leaks in the electrical current and immediately tripping to shut off the power.

Locating the GFCI. It's easy to overlook a tripped GFCI as the source of a dead outlet problem, because in areas where GFCI-protected outlets are required, electricians often connect additional standard outlets to one GFCI outlet. A current leak at any one of the outlets will trip the GFCI and cause all of the outlets connected to it to go dead. These GFCI-protected outlets are supposed to be labeled, but the label often falls off. Look for GFCIs in the bathroom, kitchen, basement, or garage and outside. Test and reset every GFCI you find.

Resetting a GFCI. If the button resets but then pops again when you turn on whatever appliance or tool you were using, it means the appliance or tool has a short. If the GFCI "reset" button doesn't pop out when you press the "test" button, there may be no power to the GFCI or you may have a bad GFCI (they eventually wear out and must be replaced). On the other hand, if the "reset" button trips again every time you press it before you've plugged anything in, there may be a dangerous current leak somewhere on the circuit. You can often diagnose the problem with a GFCI tester. Just plug it in and read the diagnosis.

FUSE HAS BLOWN

If you have fuses instead of breakers, you'll have to get a flashlight and peer into the window of each fuse until you find one that has a collapsed spring or a burned metal strip. Unscrew the fuse and replace it with a new one that has the same amp rating as the old.

Chapter 2

FIRES

Know your options and be prepared.

HOUSE FIRES— BE PREPARED

The National Fire Protection Association estimated that fire departments responded to 366,600 residence fires annually between 2007 and 2011. In 2010 home fires claimed the lives of 2,640 people and injured another 13,350 (not including firefighters). In a house fire there is no time to think about what to do and smoke fumes can be disorienting. Survival depends on split-second decisions, effective precautions, and an escape plan that everyone knows by heart.

FIRE EXTINGUISHERS

For the home, the NFPA recommends a multi-purpose extinguisher that is large enough to put out a small fire, but not so heavy as to be difficult to handle.

Use a portable fire extinguisher when the fire is confined to a small area, such as a wastebasket, and is not growing; everyone has exited the building; the fire department has been called; and the room is not filled with smoke.

TO OPERATE A FIRE EXTINGUISHER, REMEMBER THE WORD PASS:

- **P**ull the pin. Hold the extinguisher with the nozzle pointing away from you, and release the locking mechanism.

- **A**im low. Point the extinguisher at the base of the fire.

- **S**queeze the lever slowly and evenly.

- **S**weep the nozzle from side-to-side.

FIRE BLANKETS

A fire blanket is a sheet of fire-resistant material used to cover a fire to cut off the supply of oxygen. It is unlikely that you will be able to retrieve the blanket from a fire to use it again, so learn how to use it correctly the first time. You will be able to use the fire blanket more effectively if you have read the instructions.

- A fire blanket is most useful in a kitchen on small, self-contained fires, especially burning oil. It can also be used on some electrical fires or to wrap around someone whose clothes are on fire.

- Choose a blanket that is at least one yard square. Draw tapes will allow you to access the blanket quickly and enable you to hold the blanket safely between you and the fire.

- Keep the blanket accessible in a container on a wall, but not above a cooker or a heater.

- To use, cover the fire completely. Gaps allow air to get in and feed the flames. Leave the fire covered for at least 30 minutes to make sure it is fully extinguished. Discard the blanket after use and replace with a new one.

DRAW UP AN ESCAPE PLAN

1. **Involve everyone.** Plan together as a household when drawing up your fire-escape plan. Consider any special arrangements for the very young or elderly.

2. **Plan route A.** The best escape route is the one you normally use for getting in and out of the house. Keep it clear of obstructions.

3. **Plan route B.** An alternative escape route should be agreed upon and kept unobstructed, in case the first choice is blocked by the fire.

4. **Choose the refuge.** In case both escape routes are blocked, decide which room is best for your "refuge." Ensure the room can be accessed by all members of the household, especially considering anyone with mobility difficulties, and has a window that opens, facing onto a road. You will need a telephone and spare blankets or rugs.

5. **Make keys accessible.** Identify where door and window lock keys are to be kept and make sure everyone, including visitors, knows where they are.

PLAN FOR RESTRICTED MOBILITY

If there are elderly people or people with disabilities in your home, consider them in your fire-escape plan. You can ask the fire department to visit you to provide safety advice and fit specialized smoke alarms.

6. **Meeting point.** Ensure every member of the family is familiar with what should happen after they have escaped, such as meeting at a rendezvous point and contacting emergency services.

7. **Distribute the plan.** Put the plan somewhere prominent, such as on the fridge door. Conduct a fire drill to walk through the plan.

CHILDREN
Even small children should know that they must alert the household if they smell smoke or hear the smoke alarm. All children old enough to understand should know how to contact the fire department and know their address by heart. Make sure they know to call 911 only in an emergency and never in play.

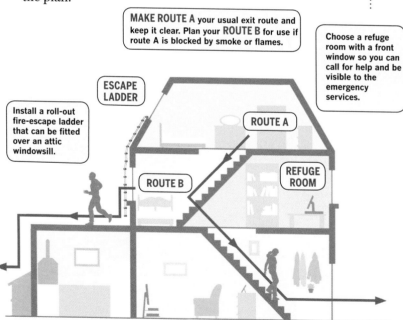

MAKE ROUTE A your usual exit route and keep it clear. Plan your ROUTE B for use if route A is blocked by smoke or flames.

Choose a refuge room with a front window so you can call for help and be visible to the emergency services.

ESCAPE LADDER

Install a roll-out fire-escape ladder that can be fitted over an attic windowsill.

ROUTE A

ROUTE B

REFUGE ROOM

If you are planning to extend your two-story home upward, you will need to abide by building regulations that set minimum standards of safety. It is likely that special fire precautions will be required, such as fire-resisting doors and partitions, to give a protected means of escape.

SMOKE ALARMS

According to the United States Fire Administration, three out of five home fire deaths result from fires in properties without working smoke alarms. Building requirements for alarms vary from locality to locality (www.ajfire.org/uploads/smoke_alarm_requirements.pdf), and you should know what is mandatory in your region.

1. **Types.** Ionization alarms detect small fast-burning fires, such as cooking fires. An optical alarm detects slow-burning fires, such as smoldering furniture. Install at least one of each type, or invest in a combined alarm.

2. **Power.** Most smoke alarms use a 9V battery. Standard batteries should be replaced every 12 months. Hardwired smoke alarms, with a battery backup in case of power failure, must be installed by a qualified electrician.

3. **Light options.** Some alarms are fitted with a light that comes on as the alarm sounds, in case damage to electrical wiring affects the house lighting.

4. **Operating light.** A slowly pulsing small light is visible when the alarm is on, and will flash more rapidly when the alarm sounds.

5. **Maintenance.** All smoke alarms have a manual test facility. Press the button weekly to check the alarm, or shine a flashlight beam over those with a flashlight test facility. Most alarms will "chirp" for the last 30 days of battery life. Change the battery immediately.

KITCHEN FIRES

The most common cooking fires, the leading cause of residential building fires, are caused by deep-fat frying.

OIL FIRES

1. **Leave the pan on the stove.** Do not attempt to move a burning pan. Instead, cover it with the lid, unless the fire is too large.

2. **Turn off the heat.** Only do this at the stove if it is safe to do so. If you have to reach across the fire to do this, turn off the appliance at the power source.

3. **Get out.** Leave the kitchen and close the door. Get everyone out of the house and call 911.

MICROWAVE FIRES

Most microwave fires are caused through misuse. Never use for drying clothes and do not place any metal objects inside.

1. **Keep the oven door closed.** Opening the door will allow oxygen inside to feed the fire so keep the door closed. Switch off the power if it is safe to do so.

2. **Prevent flames from spreading.** Throw a fire blanket over the microwave to contain and put out the flames.

GENERAL HINTS AND TIPS

- Clean toasters regularly and keep them away from curtains.

- Turn off cooking appliances after use.

- Keep pets and small children at least one yard away from the stove.

- Take particular care if you are wearing loose clothing, as it can easily catch fire.

CHIMNEY FIRES

There are around 25,000 chimney fires a year in the United States. Although a chimney is built to cope with a fire, chimney fires can spread into the attic space or under floors and may cause extensive damage to the fabric of the whole house.

The buildup of soot or tar deposits is heated by a lit fire from below and can itself ignite, with the resulting fire spreading up the chimney. One of the first indications of a chimney fire from inside the house is a roaring sound from the chimney. On the outside you will be able to see thick clouds of smoke and there may be flames coming out of the chimney.

1. **Call 911 immediately.**

2. **Reduce oxygen supply.** If you have an enclosed stove, shut all air vents and flue dampers to deprive the fire of oxygen.

3. **Move furniture.** To avoid further risk, move furniture away from the fireplace. This should be done in any room that shares the chimney.

4. **Insure free access.** Make sure the fire department has access to the attic space.

5. **Hose down the roof.** Hose down the roof around the chimney with water, but avoid the chimney itself.

The chimney itself can reach temperatures that are high enough to ignite neighboring timber in the loft or under floorboards. The extreme heat makes the chimney expand, which can cause nearby plaster to crack and cause structural damage.

FOR NEXT TIME . . .

- Chimneys should be cleaned at least once a year—twice if you are burning soft woods. Your insurance company may not pay out for chimney fire damage if this has not been done.

- Use a chimney-cleaning additive or a chimney cleaning log to help dry out the accumulated tar so it flakes off. This should be done a week or so before the chimney is swept.

- Only use well-seasoned wood for burning. Never burn cardboard or Christmas trees.

- Do not use your fire as a wastepaper bin.

- Use only recommended fuels.

- Have small, frequent "hot" fires that burn more completely and produce less smoke.

- Burning wood produces a lot of soot and tar, so if you have an enclosed fire, such as a wood-burning stove or kitchen stove, ensure it is connected to a properly insulated chimney liner. It needs a flue pipe connected to a double-wall stainless steel liner or a lightweight concrete liner. Make sure flues are professionally installed for safety.

CANDLE OR CIGARETTE FIRE

1. **Assess the fire.** If a cigarette, unextinguished cigar/cigarette butt, or fallen candle causes a fire, ascertain what is on fire in order to take the appropriate action.

   - **Burning plastic:** Night lights can get hot enough to melt plastic, which can then ignite. Use a dry powder fire extinguisher (see page 31) to put out fires involving burning plastic.

   - **Burning curtains:** Use water to extinguish burning curtains—throw water onto the fabric from a bucket, or for a smaller fire, pour water from a jug or kettle. Use a fire extinguisher, if available.

   - **Smoldering upholstery:** Use water from a bucket or bowl to douse upholstery. Use a fire extinguisher, if available. If possible, take the furniture outside in case a deep-seated fire continues to smolder and ignites later.

2. **Get out and stay out.** If any fire takes hold and is no longer localized, get everyone out of the house and call 911. Stay out.

USING CANDLES SAFELY

- Never leave a burning candle unattended.

- Use a snuffer or spoon to put it out. Blowing could spread sparks and hot wax. Do not move it.

- Keep candles out of drafts and away from curtains and other fabrics or furniture.

- Keep clothes and your hair away from the candle's flame.

- Do not drop anything, such as a matchstick, into hot wax, as the candle may flare up.

- Stand candles on a heat-resistant surface in a secure and stable holder so they do not fall over.

SMOKING PRECAUTIONS

- Never leave a burning cigarette unattended.

- Put a cigarette out properly—never discard a lit butt end. Cigarettes burn at 1,292°F (700°C) and contain chemicals designed to keep them alight.

- Never smoke in bed or when drowsy.

IF YOUR CLOTHES CATCH FIRE

1. **Stop, drop, and roll.** Moving around will fan the flames and make them burn faster. Dropping to the ground and rolling around will stop the fire from spreading and engulfing you. Since flames burn upward, lying down will also help to protect your face and head.

2. **Smother the flames.** To be even more effective, wrap yourself in a fire blanket, heavy coat or thick blanket.

ELECTRICAL FIRES

There are various signs of potential electrical problems. These include fuses that "blow" frequently, flickering lights, and scorch marks on sockets or plugs.

1. **Turn OFF the electricity.** This needs to be done at the main supply at the circuit breaker. Do not touch or remove the plug or appliances until the electricity is turned off to avoid the possibility of an electric shock.

2. **Extinguish fire.** Use a fire blanket or a dry powder or carbon dioxide fire extinguisher on small electrical fires. Never use water, as it could cause electrocution.

3. **Get help.** If you cannot put out the fire get out of the property and call 911 immediately.

GENERAL HINTS AND TIPS

- Never overload an adapter for single appliances or trailing adapters with several socket outlets.

- Use an extension cord rated for appliances and tools. If you use a thin, light-gauge cord for an electric heater or large appliance, the cord will overheat. If in doubt, use a heavier extension cord.

- Electrical appliances should be serviced once a year—especially those with heaters and motors.

- Electric blankets should be checked annually and not left on all night unless they are blankets designed for continuous running.

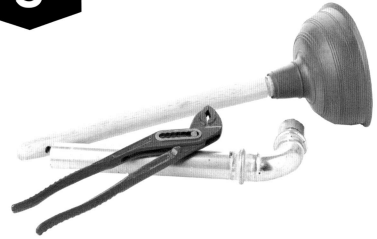

Chapter

3

PLUMBING
AND WATER ISSUES

Fix what you can to keep damage down to a minimum.

WATER COMING THROUGH CEILING

When water comes through a ceiling you must act fast to avoid costly structural repairs, as well as serious damage to decorations, furnishings, and floor coverings. There can be many causes: the roof may be damaged, a water tank in an attic may have split, a bathtub may be overflowing, or a washing machine in an apartment above may be leaking.

WATER THROUGH CEILING

1. **Turn off the electricity.** Water can pose a risk of electrocution as well as damaging wiring circuits above the ceiling. Turn off the circuit breakers for electrical circuits in the area of the leak. Keep a flashlight or two around the house so you can find your way in the dark.

2. **Catch the water.** Place empty buckets to catch the water so that you can save your flooring. Do not use garbage cans to catch the water, because you will be unable to lift them when they are full.

3. **Turn off the water.** If the water is caused by a plumbing problem (see assessment, opposite), turn it off.

CEILING IS BULGING

1. **Prepare to catch the water.** If the ceiling is bulging, you need to take action before it collapses. Start by putting a waterproof covering down, such as a polythene sheet, and then place a large bucket underneath the bulge to catch the water. Have spare buckets or similar-sized containers standing by.

ASSESSMENT

First do the "Water Through Ceiling" action steps (see opposite), then identify
where the water is coming from. If you cannot perform the procedures yourself,
seek professional help.

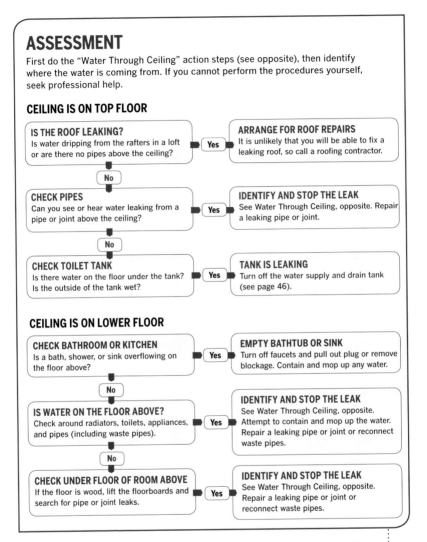

CEILING IS ON TOP FLOOR

IS THE ROOF LEAKING?
Is water dripping from the rafters in a loft
or are there no pipes above the ceiling?

Yes → **ARRANGE FOR ROOF REPAIRS**
It is unlikely that you will be able to fix a
leaking roof, so call a roofing contractor.

No ↓

CHECK PIPES
Can you see or hear water leaking from a
pipe or joint above the ceiling?

Yes → **IDENTIFY AND STOP THE LEAK**
See Water Through Ceiling, opposite. Repair
a leaking pipe or joint.

No ↓

CHECK TOILET TANK
Is there water on the floor under the tank?
Is the outside of the tank wet?

Yes → **TANK IS LEAKING**
Turn off the water supply and drain tank
(see page 46).

CEILING IS ON LOWER FLOOR

CHECK BATHROOM OR KITCHEN
Is a bath, shower, or sink overflowing on
the floor above?

Yes → **EMPTY BATHTUB OR SINK**
Turn off faucets and pull out plug or remove
blockage. Contain and mop up any water.

No ↓

IS WATER ON THE FLOOR ABOVE?
Check around radiators, toilets, appliances,
and pipes (including waste pipes).

Yes → **IDENTIFY AND STOP THE LEAK**
See Water Through Ceiling, opposite.
Attempt to contain and mop up the water.
Repair a leaking pipe or joint or reconnect
waste pipes.

No ↓

CHECK UNDER FLOOR OF ROOM ABOVE
If the floor is wood, lift the floorboards and
search for pipe or joint leaks.

Yes → **IDENTIFY AND STOP THE LEAK**
See Water Through Ceiling, opposite.
Repair a leaking pipe or joint or
reconnect waste pipes.

2. **Make a drainage hole.** Use a pointed stick to make a hole
   in the middle of a large bulge to let the water through.

3. **Prop up damaged sections.** If it looks as though part of
   the ceiling is about to come down, make a temporary prop
   with a length of wood, wedged between two short planks of
   wood—one on the floor and one on the ceiling—to hold it up.

LEAKY PLUMBING

1. **Turn off main shutoff.** Turn off the water at the main shutoff valve (see page 51).

2. **Drain the water lines.** If you need to shut off the water supply to the house to make repairs, open all the faucets (after you've shut off the water) throughout the house so that the water in the pipes will drain out at the lowest point, instead of draining out on you when you cut the pipe to make repairs.

TOILET TANK LEAKING

1. **Close the shutoff valve under the toilet.** If the shutoff leaks (often the case with old, standard-type shutoffs), turn off the main shutoff and replace the toilet shutoff with a ball valve shutoff.

2. **Drain tank.** Flush the toilet to empty it quickly and minimize the amount of water that can leak from it. Call a plumber to repair or replace the tank.

APPLIANCE LEAK

Switch off appliance. If a washing machine or dishwasher is leaking, pull the plug, then turn off its water supply at the shutoffs at the end of the machine's inlet hose or hoses. Call a repairman.

WHAT NEXT?

• Call in a contractor to inspect the ceiling to see if it needs repairing or replacing.

• If you live in an apartment with neighbors above, ask if you can keep a set of their keys. If water comes through your ceiling when they are out, you can get in and take appropriate action. Keep their cell phone number to let them know of any problem.

BURST AND LEAKING PIPES

Pipes will burst or their joints be forced apart as ice that has frozen inside begins to thaw. You can prevent pipes from freezing in the first place by insulating them effectively, but it is possible to stop a pipe from bursting if you thaw it in the correct way. A leaking pipe or joint may also be the result of other problems, such as damage or corrosion.

TYPES OF PIPE

- A copper pipe is the most common and is easily split by ice. It can be repaired with a clamp, a "slip" coupling, or a new section of pipe.

- A galvanized pipe that freezes and leaks can be difficult to repair if it's rusted or corroded (often the case). Replace the damaged section with PEX, copper, or CPVC.

- PEX or CPVC pipe is the least likely to split and easiest to repair (with a new section).

BURST AND FROZEN PIPES

- Burst pipes are caused by water freezing in pipes. Exterior walls and unheated crawlspaces and basements are the most likely places for burst pipes.

- In cold weather, no water coming from a tap indicates a frozen pipe. This must be dealt with swiftly, as the pipe could burst.

LEAKING PIPE OR JOINT

- The first sign of a leaking pipe or pipe joint is likely to be a damp patch on a wall or ceiling. Such a leak may be just a dribble, but must be mended before too much damage is done.

- A separated waste pipe joint can leak out a lot of water and must be reconnected quickly.

PREVENT PIPES FREEZING

- **Insulate.** Pipes in exterior walls, crawlspaces, or outside should be properly insulated. Wrap pipes in insulation, build chases with rigid insulation, or heat the space that the pipe runs through.

- **Heating.** Leave the heating on low if you are away in winter; for long absences, turn off the water and drain the system.

- **Waste pipes.** A buildup of frozen water in a drainpipe may not split the pipe, but it can cause clogs. Make sure pipes in cold parts of the house drain properly.

WATER IS LEAKING

1. **Turn off the electricity.** First, turn off the electricity at the circuit breaker. Take a flashlight if it is dark. Water leaking from pipes or pipe joints can get into electrical fittings (especially ceiling fixtures and junction boxes), making them unsafe.

2. **Locate the leak.** Find the source of the leak as quickly as possible. Do not turn the water off until you have located the problem.

3. **Turn off the water.** Turn off the water at the main shutoff or the shutoff controlling the leaking section of pipe. If it is a hot-water or central-heating pipe that has burst, switch off the boiler or hot water heater.

BURST PIPE

- With a burst or split copper pipe, you can use a "slip" coupling (which has no internal pipe stop and so can be used on pipes in situ). Cut out the affected section and slide on the slip coupling. Call a plumber if you are not confident about doing this yourself.

- The simplest way to temporarily stop water leaking from a burst or split pipe is to use an emergency pipe repair clamp (see illustration), screwed in place over the leak.

FROZEN PIPE

1. **Identify the pipe.** If all the faucets are affected, the frozen spot is somewhere in the main supply line. If only one or two faucets are affected, check the pipes feeding them.

2. **Melt the ice.** Ask a helper to open each affected faucet, while you work backward along the pipe leading to it. Remove any pipe insulation first. If the pipe is made of copper or galvanized steel, use a hair dryer to heat it until water flows freely from the faucet. Treat plastic water pipes in the same way as plastic waste pipes (see below).

3. **Use hot towels.** If plastic waste pipes are frozen, soak towels in hot water and wrap them around the pipe until the wastewater flows away.

LEAKING JOINT

- **Tighten compression joint.** If a compression joint is leaking, the leak can normally be stopped by tightening one or both nuts. Always use two wrenches, one on the nut and one on the fitting.

- **Replace soldered joint.** A leaking soldered joint is difficult to repair. Cut out the affected joint and replace it with a new coupling or pipe.

- **Replace plastic pipe fittings.** If the joint is a compression fitting, try tightening it. If it's welded or a PEX fitting, replace it.

- **Fix the drain assembly.** If one of the joints in a drain assembly under the kitchen or bathroom sink is leaking, unscrew the slip nut, push the pipe back in, and retighten the slip nut. If the washer looks damaged, replace it. Don't overtighten.

- **Tighten radiator nut.** Leaks from radiators can usually be cured by tightening the "union" nut—the one closest to the radiator at the bottom.

WHAT NEXT?

- If the repairs are temporary, call in a plumber to make permanent repairs.

- Assess the results of the leak or burst and contact your insurance company if ceilings, floor coverings, or wallpaper have been damaged.

- Ask an electrician to check the electric wiring before turning the electricity back on.

- Rent a dehumidifier to dry out the property.

Where to turn off the water

MAIN SHUTOFF

This valve controls the flow of water into your home from the water main. It is usually found where the water supply enters the house, and there are usually two of them—one on each side of the water meter. Turn it clockwise to shut off the water.

TANK GATE VALVE

A gate valve controls the flow from a cold-water tank. Gate valves often have red or orange handles and are usually found near where a pipe leaves the tank at its base. Cold-water tanks are extremely rare.

Leaking pipe

Wrap it up. A temporary fix for a leaking pipe is to wrap self-amalgamating (Alfa) tape tightly over the leaking section (no need to turn the water off first). The layers of tape will merge and create a fully waterproof seal, even on pipes with water at main pressure.

FLOODED BASEMENT

Water entering a basement or cellar usually has nowhere to go: it just collects and ruins anything you keep down there, and it will probably leave behind an unpleasant smell. There are a number of things you can do to make some types of minor flooding less likely, but tackling a proper flood is a difficult and often dirty job.

Serious basement flooding is usually the result of an "outside agency"—typically heavy rainfall or flooding from nearby streams or rivers. Flooding can also be the result of water seeping in through the basement or cellar walls or through the floor. The best solution for this problem is interior drain tile and a sump pump. This is expensive, but if you use your cellar for storage you may decide it is worthwhile.

FLOODING FROM LEAKY PIPE

1. **Turn off the water.** If the cause of the cellar flood is a burst or leaking pipe, turn off the water.

2. **Catch the water.** If possible put a bucket under the leak to catch the water. Have several containers standing by until all the water has drained from the pipe, which might take some time even after you have turned off the water.

3. **Protect possessions.** Get anything at risk from damage by the water out of the cellar quickly. Call a plumber to have the pipe repaired.

4. **Pump out the water.** Unless your flood is of fire-department proportions (usually when it occurs from an outside source—see opposite), rent a submersible pump, which will remove all except the last few puddles of water

(the remainder can be sucked up with a wet/dry vacuum cleaner).

FLOODING FROM OUTSIDE

1. **Use sandbags.** If you are threatened by excessive rainfall, overflowing rivers, or a burst water main, sandbags will stop water getting in under doors—but not for long.

2. **Save valuables.** With localized flooding or a burst water main in the street, you should have sufficient warning to give you time to move at least some of your cherished items out of the basement or ground floor.

3. **Call emergency services.** If the basement or cellar is inundated, a plumber can come and pump it out.

BLOCKED SINK OR BATHTUB

When water will not drain away from a sink or bathtub, the most likely cause is a blockage in the trap or in the waste pipes under or behind the sink (or bathtub, shower, or bidet). If you have the right tools, you can clear the blockage yourself. In winter, the blockage may be due to a frozen waste pipe outside.

PREVENTION

- Avoid putting either grease or fat down the drain in kitchen sinks—they solidify and block the waste.

- Similarly, avoid flushing food scraps down the sink and use a drain strainer. If food does go down the drain, run the water to rinse it away well.

- In bathtubs, sinks, and shower trays, human hair is the main problem—pick out loose strands whenever you see them.

- To keep waste pipes clear, pour a cupful of baking soda (bicarbonate of soda) crystals down the drain once a month (once a week for sinks).

- If the flow from a waste pipe has slowed down, attend to it as soon as you can before it gets fully blocked.

1. **Remove visible obstructions.** Use fingers and tweezers (or a straightened-out metal coat hanger) to pull out any bits you can see.

2. **Use a plunger.** Use a wet cloth to block the overflow, fit the rubber cup of a sink plunger over the drain, and pump

the handle sharply up and down. Repeat this several times until the waste is clear.

3. **Blow it out.** If you use an aerosol clearer, which uses a blast of air to shift the blockage, follow the manufacturer's instructions.

4. **Remove trap.** Place a bucket underneath the trap and unscrew the slip nuts to remove the trap. Clean the trap out in another sink or in a bucket—remember that you cannot use a sink while the trap is in pieces.

5. **Clear pipe.** If the blockage is not in the trap, but is farther along the waste pipe, use a sink augur (plumber's snake) to wiggle it out.

Partly blocked waste pipe

PROTECT OUTLET
Chemical drain cleaners can be used if waste pipes are slow to clear. To protect the waste pipe outlet from attack by the aggressive chemicals, smear petroleum jelly (Vaseline) over it first.

POUR IN CHEMICAL CLEANER
Wearing gloves, pour the chemical cleaner down the drain, following the instructions. Do not use chemicals to clear a totally blocked waste pipe, as these might not wash away and may consequently leave a dangerous liquid in your sink or bathtub.

BLOCKED DRAINS

The homeowner is responsible for all external pipes and drains up until they join a public sewer. Therefore, it is important to know how to deal with a blocked drain. This can help to avoid emergency charges for problems that you can deal with easily yourself, although if you are not able to do so, contact a professional.

Drains rarely get blocked suddenly. If they are beginning to slow down, take action to clean them out before they become completely blocked. If a blockage or leak is persistent, a drain-clearing firm can send tiny cameras along your drains to check for cracks and to find blockages such as tree roots.

ASSESSMENT

Clogs can occur in the waste lines below sinks and toilets or anywhere in the main waste line as it goes through the house and out to the street. Any clogs before the waste line empties into the sewer line in the street are the homeowner's responsibility. Look for the following signs:

PROBLEM	WHAT TO DO
SOME FIXTURES DRAIN SLOWLY There's a partial clog in one of the branch waste lines before it joins the main waste line.	**CLEAR WASTE LINE** Remove the highest sink drain pipe and push a snake down into the main waste line util you find a clog.
ALL THE FIXTURES DRAIN SLOWLY There's a partial clog in the main waste line between the last fixture and the sewer line in the street.	**CLEAR THE CLEANOUT PLUG** Open the cleanout plug in the basement or bottom level and push a long snake in.
WATER COMING OUT OF BASEMENT DRAIN Water coming out of the lowest drain or fixture means the main waste line is completely clogged.	**CLEAR THE MAIN WASTE LINE** Rent a power drain-cleaning machine or call a pro. There may be roots blocking the waste line.

CLOGGED WASTE LINE

If you can't find a clog in the drain or trap under the fixture that's backing up, then the clog is somewhere in the waste line. The first access point to try is through the pipe under the sink or tub. You'll need to use a plumbing snake at this point. Plumbing snakes are lengths of tightly wound wire that are highly flexible so they can go around sharp 90-degree bends in drain lines. A 15- to 20-footer that's 1/4 in. thick will handle most household needs. They're available at all hardware stores and home centers. Expect the snake to take 20 to 30 minutes. You'll have to shove the snake down the drain, spinning it around corners and into clogs. The corkscrew tip grabs obstructions so you can pull them out, or breaks through them.

USING A SNAKE

1. **Uncoil the snake and lay it out straight.** Otherwise it'll suddenly spring out when you release the coil.

2. **Shove the snake firmly into the drain.** Twist it at the same time to get around tough corners.

3. **Turn the snake clockwise when you feel resistance, so it winds into obstructions.** Then pull back slightly. If you feel resistance, you've hooked into something. Pull it out.

4. **If the snake continues to make progress (extends deeper into the drain), stick with it.** It'll slowly chew through tough stuff. You won't know for sure that you've solved the problem until you reassemble the drain and run water through it. So run the snake in as far as you can.

5. **Drains are dirty.** Wipe the goop off the snake with a rag as you pull it out.

FINDING THE CLOG

1. **Remove the drain lines under the sink.** Push the snake into the drain line, making sure it heads downhill into the waste line. Continue pushing it until you find the clog or run out of snake. Reassemble everything and see if it drains.

2. **If the water still doesn't drain, try the next access point you can get to.** This will most often be the cleanout plug in the basement or ground floor where the waste line makes a horizontal turn. If the water is not draining at all, get some buckets and rags and sponges ready in case water comes out. Wear rubber gloves.

3. **Work your way downstream if there's more than one cleanout.** If that doesn't work, you'll have to rent a drain cleaning machine with a long cable and special heads for cutting through whatever is blocking the pipe. At this point it's usually easier to call in a service that specializes in cleaning drains. They'll also be better able to diagnose the problem that caused the clog in the first place.

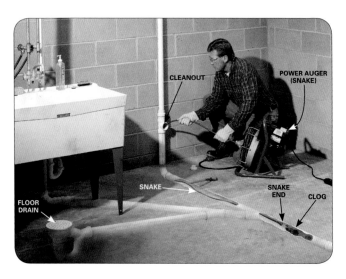

Know your DWV system

The drain, waste, and vent system carries waste out of your house and into the sewer lines or septic tank. Every drain must have a trap, and every trap must have a vent. The water in the trap keeps sewer gas from flowing into your house. Without a vent, water flowing through a trap creates a vacuum and siphons the trap dry. Vents act as a vacuum breaker, and if you notice water in the traps bubbling or being sucked out, there may be a blockage or improper venting, though this is not common.

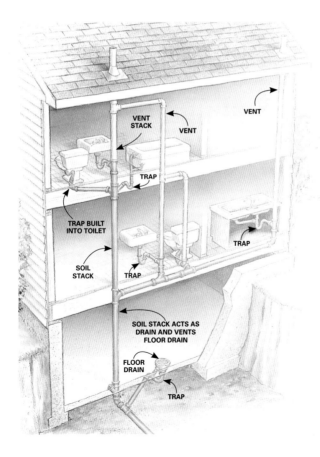

VENT STACK

VENT

VENT

TRAP

TRAP BUILT INTO TOILET

TRAP

SOIL STACK

TRAP

SOIL STACK ACTS AS DRAIN AND VENTS FLOOR DRAIN

FLOOR DRAIN

TRAP

TOILET BLOCKED OR WILL NOT FLUSH

A toilet that will not flush is a problem that needs to be sorted out as soon as possible—especially if there are young children or older people in the home. As an emergency measure you can get the contents of the toilet to go away by pouring a bucket of water into the bowl. But you need to find out what caused the problem and how to make repairs.

If you notice the toilet starting to empty more slowly than usual, use a plunger (or an aerosol air blaster) to clear the blockage that is starting to form. For all toilet repairs, wear protective clothing (heavy-duty waterproof gloves with long cuffs) and cover the floor with old towels. Disinfect equipment after use. If you do not feel able to mend a non-flushing tank or to clear a blockage in the toilet, contact a plumber to do it for you.

ASSESSMENT

Follow the chart below to find out what may be preventing the toilet bowl from emptying. Then either unblock it or fix the flush yourself or call an emergency plumber.

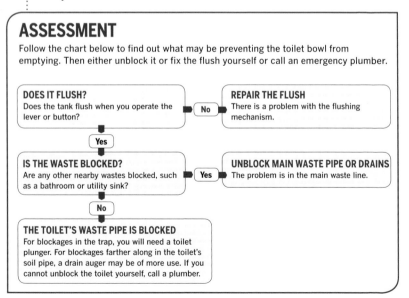

DOES IT FLUSH?
Does the tank flush when you operate the lever or button?

No → **REPAIR THE FLUSH**
There is a problem with the flushing mechanism.

Yes

IS THE WASTE BLOCKED?
Are any other nearby wastes blocked, such as a bathroom or utility sink?

Yes → **UNBLOCK MAIN WASTE PIPE OR DRAINS**
The problem is in the main waste line.

No

THE TOILET'S WASTE PIPE IS BLOCKED
For blockages in the trap, you will need a toilet plunger. For blockages farther along in the toilet's soil pipe, a drain auger may be of more use. If you cannot unblock the toilet yourself, call a plumber.

How a toilet works

FLUSH HANDLE

When you push the flush handle, you raise the flapper and all the water in the tank gushes into the bowl. Then the flapper closes and the tank refills.

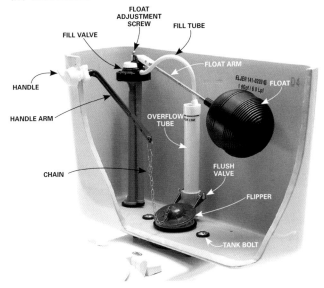

FILL VALVE

After a flush, the lowered float opens this valve to refill the tank. When the fill valve doesn't close completely the toilet runs constantly.

OVERFLOW TUBE

The overflow tube prevents the tank from overflowing if the fill valve doesn't close.

FILL TUBE

After a flush, most of the water passing through the fill valve refills the tank, but some of the water runs through the fill tube and through the overflow to refill the tank.

REPAIR THE FILL VALVE

1. **Adjust the float.** Gently bend the float arm down to put extra pressure on the valve and make it close sooner.

2. **If bending the float arm doesn't work, replace the fill valve.** Turn off the water at the main shutoff and drain the tank. Replace the shutoff and supply line if they're old. Then install the new fill valve. Follow the instructions that came with it to adjust it. Hand-tighten the supply line.

REPLACE THE FLAPPER

1. **Disconnect the flapper.** Unhook the chain and disconnect the flapper from the ears on the overflow tube.

2. **Install a new flapper.** Take the old one to the hardware store and find a match or a universal flapper. Fit the new flapper on and reconnect the chain.

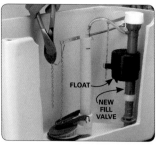

ADJUST THE CHAIN

- Move the clip to a different link. The chain should have just a little slack when the flapper is closed. If the chain is too long, you'll have to hold the handle down to get a complete flush. If it's too short, the flapper won't seal. If the chain is much longer than necessary, cut off the excess to avoid tangles.

ADJUST THE FILL HEIGHT

- Slide the float up or down. If the water level is too low, you'll get a weak flush. If it's too high, water will spill over the overflow tube and the toilet will run constantly. To adjust this type of float, just pinch the clip and move it up or down.

CLEARING A CLOG

1. **Use a plunger with a fold-out flange.** It will seal better around the toilet drain for a more powerful plunge. Start gently. Before the first push, the plunger is full of air, so a hard push will blast sewage water out of the bowl. bowl. Increase the force of the plunge after the air is all pushed out. Don't give up—it may take 20 pushes or more to clear a clog. If you need more water, refill the bowl by lifting the flapper in the tank, or the plunger won't work.

2. **If the plunger won't work, use a closet auger.** An auger is a type of snake with a rubber sleeve to protect the bowl from marks. Insert the snake and turn the handle. As it twists deeper  into the drain (push hard!), the corkscrew tip will either break the clog or snag it and pull it out.

MEDICAL EMERGENCIES AND FIRST AID

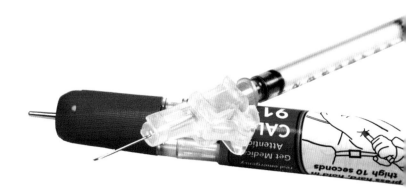

MEDICAL
EMERGENCIES

Early treatment can be a lifesaver.

ABDOMINAL ISSUES

SEVERE ABDOMINAL PAIN

Most abdominal pain is short-lived and is caused by a minor ailment such as indigestion or mild food poisoning. Severe abdominal pain can result from injury or be a sign of a more serious disorder affecting the digestive system, urinary system, or, in women, of the reproductive system. Persistent or severe abdominal pain needs prompt medical attention.

Pain anywhere in the abdomen may be localized or general. Find out as much detail as you can, as it helps the medical team. Ask the patient when she last ate or drank something. If you suspect serious illness or injury, do not give the patient anything to eat or drink (including pain relief medication), as he may need an anesthetic later.

SYMPTOMS

- Possible fever and/or generally feeling unwell

- Bleeding (internal or external) if pain results from an injury

- Bloating or distended abdomen

- Vomiting and/or diarrhea—if together and either prolonged or severe

- Urinary problems

- Symptoms and signs of shock (see page 107)

IS IT SERIOUS?

SIGNS	QUESTIONS TO ASK
PAIN	Has this happened before? Where is the pain? Is it concentrated in one area or has it spread? If so, where? Is it mild, moderate, or severe—ask the patient to give it a score out of 10. Is the pain continuous or intermittent and has it changed or moved? When and where did it start? Does movement, breathing, or coughing make it worse (or better)?
BLEEDING	Where is the bleeding? Is blood loss slight or severe? Are there signs of internal bleeding (see page 107)?
VOMITING	How many times has the patient vomited and when did it start? Does she feel better after vomiting? What does the vomit look like? Does it contain dark reddish blood that looks like coffee grounds?
DIARRHEA	How often do the bouts of diarrhea occur? Does the patient feel better after going to the toilet? Is there blood in the feces?
URINE	When did the patient last urinate and was it normal? Was it painful? Is the urine normal or cloudy? Does it smell unusual and/or contain blood?
ADDITIONAL SYMPTOMS	Does the patient have a fever? Is she restless or tired, or is she too weak to move? Could she have food poisoning or has she been in contact with anyone who has gastroenteritis? Is the patient a woman of child-bearing age? Does she have a history of menstrual pain? Could she be pregnant?

1. **Make patient comfortable.** Sit or lie her down. She may be most comfortable if she is propped up with pillows. Give her a bowl if she is feeling sick.

2. **Give a hot-water bottle.** Wrap a hot-water bottle in a towel and give it (or a heating pad)to the patient to hold against her stomach.

3. **Seek medical advice.** If you are in any doubt about the patient's condition, seek medical advice. Make a note of her level of consciousness, breathing, and pulse. If her condition deteriorates, call emergency services.

WARNING

Call emergency services immediately if there is an obvious abdominal wound or if the pain lasts more than four hours in an adult (one hour in a child) and is accompanied by ANY of the following:

- Severe vomiting and/or diarrhea.

- Blood-stained vomit.

- Swollen and tender abdomen.

- Swelling in the groin or scrotum.

- Patient feels faint and confused.

- Fresh, bright red blood from the anus or dark, tarry stools.

- Blood in the urine.

- Severe pain and heavy bleeding in early pregnancy could be a sign of miscarriage or a life-threatening ectopic pregnancy in which the fetus develops outside the womb and requires urgent medical treatment.

Appendicitis

Appendicitis is an inflamed appendix. The appendix is a small blind-ended tube attached to the first section of the large intestine. It is situated on the lower right-hand side of the abdomen.

- **Appendicitis can be serious.** It is a common cause of abdominal pain, especially in children. The appendix can become inflamed, swollen, and infected. This can lead to gangrene (tissue death) in the wall of the appendix, which may burst as a result.

- **Diagnosis and treatment:** The pain usually begins in the center of the abdomen. Over a period of hours it worsens and becomes most intense in the lower right-hand side. The patient needs to be admitted to the hospital for surgery. If the appendix bursts, the pain may suddenly stop, but this can lead to the life-threatening infection, peritonitis (inflammation of the membranes lining the abdominal cavity and covering the organs).

VOMITING

Caused by irritation of the digestive system, vomiting can result from a viral or bacterial infection or parasites. If prolonged, it can cause dehydration, and the risk is greater when diarrhea and vomiting occur together. Most cases of vomiting are mild, but if symptoms are severe or the person is young, elderly, or has another illness, hospital treatment may be needed. Nausea, vomiting, and tiredness are common during early pregnancy.

Prolonged vomiting and diarrhea in elderly people, young children, and babies can have serious health consequences, and they have a greater risk of becoming dehydrated.

ELDERLY PEOPLE

- Most elderly people can be treated at home. Make the patient comfortable and treat as indicated on page 72, but monitor the patient for signs of dehydration—headache, dry mouth and eyes, thirst, muscle weakness—as this can be fatal.

- Give the patient plenty of water to drink, on its own or with rehydration salts. Some types of rehydration salts are not suitable for people with a kidney condition. Always check the package instructions.

- If the vomiting in an elderly person is severe, prolonged, and/or accompanied by diarrhea, call for medical advice. If the patient shows signs of dehydration, he may need to be taken to the hospital for treatment.

BABIES AND YOUNG CHILDREN

- If a baby is breastfed, advise the mother to keep breastfeeding to replace lost fluid. A baby who is bottle-fed should be given water or water with rehydration salts.

- Call for medical advice if a baby or young child keeps vomiting most of his feeds or has watery stools; vomiting or diarrhea lasts more than eight hours in a baby (or 24 hours in a young child); there are signs of dehydration, such as sunken eyes and/or fontanel in a baby. If a baby or young child is vomiting and has diarrhea, call for medical advice even sooner, as the risk of dehydration is greater.

TREATING A VOMITING PATIENT

1. **Make comfortable.** Reassure the patient and make him as comfortable as possible. Give him a cloth to wipe his face.

2. **Give sips of water.** Give the patient water after he has been sick. Tell him to sip the water slowly, as he may vomit again.

3. **Build up fluids.** Gradually build up the amount of fluid he drinks. Water is sufficient, but you can give him water containing rehydration salts (follow the package instructions) or unsweetened fruit juice.

4. **Introduce food gradually.** When the patient is beginning to feel hungry again, give him small amounts of easily digested foods. Try plain pasta, rice, or bread for the first 24 hours. If vomiting persists or recurs or there are other symptoms, such as diarrhea, seek medical advice.

FOOD POISONING

Eating food or drink that is contaminated with bacteria or the toxins that it produces can cause food poisoning. Some bacteria, commonly Campylobacter, E. coli, and Salmonella, multiply fast in food in warm, damp conditions. The more bacteria are present, the higher the chance of infection and illness. Most bacteria are destroyed by thorough cooking; food poisoning can result from eating undercooked foods.

- **Reporting incidents.** Food poisoning can affect a whole group if they have all eaten the same contaminated food. Severe cases should be reported to the local health authority so that the source can be identified.

- **When to seek advice.** Most cases of food poisoning clear up within a few days without medical treatment. Seek medical advice if the vomiting or diarrhea lasts for more than a few days or the condition worsens, there is blood in the stools, the diarrhea contains yellowish or greenish mucus, or the affected person is elderly, pregnant, or a baby or young child.

DIARRHEA

If a patient passes watery stools more than three times a day, he has diarrhea. Diarrhea may accompany vomiting or it may occur on its own. As with vomiting, it is generally a symptom of an infection, such as food poisoning. Diarrhea usually clears up in a couple of days and is not serious. There is a risk of dehydration if diarrhea persists. If a patient has chronic diarrhea that lasts for more than two weeks, it is most likely to be the symptom of a long-term condition such as irritable bowel syndrome.

1. **Give sips of water.** Give him water to drink to replace some of the lost fluids and tell him to sip it slowly. He should aim to drink about a cup of fluid after every loose stool.

2. **Build up fluids.** Gradually build up the amount of fluid that he drinks. Water is sufficient, but you can give him water containing rehydration salts. Avoid sports drinks or sugary drinks, as the sugar content can make diarrhea worse.

3. **Introduce food gradually.** When the patient is beginning to feel hungry again, give him small amounts of easily digested foods. Offer foods such as plain pasta, rice, or bread for the first 24 hours. If diarrhea persists or recurs or there is blood in the stools, seek medical advice.

ALLERGIC REACTION

Any allergic reaction, including the most extreme form, occurs because the body's immune system reacts inappropriately in response to the presence of a substance that it wrongly perceives as a threat. There may only be mild itching, a skin rash, wheezing or sneezing, or, more rarely, a whole-body reaction—anaphylaxis.

Symptoms of allergy are commonly mild, but a severe allergic reaction is life-threatening and occurs within seconds or minutes of exposure to the allergen. In a severe allergy, many of the features of mild allergy are present, but more pronounced. Look out for the following signs or symptoms:

MILD ALLERGIC REACTION

- Red, itchy rash, possibly blotchy with raised red areas of skin (hives)

- Swollen, puffy hands and feet

- Sneezing and possible wheezing

- History of mild allergy

- Possible abdominal pain and/or vomiting

- Itchy, watery eyes, often reddened

SEVERE ALLERGIC REACTION

- Initially, generalized flushed appearance to the skin, possibly all over the body

- Swelling of the mouth and throat

- Difficulty breathing and possible asthma attack in a susceptible patient, who may gasp for air

- Difficulty swallowing, which gradually worsens

- The patient feels a sense of impending doom and may become very agitated, confused, and frightened

- Patient feels weak as blood pressure drops, and skin becomes pale; possible collapse

A severe allergic reaction is life-threatening. Occasionally a serious reaction to a known allergen takes several hours to develop. If in doubt, call for emergency help. Common triggers of mild allergy are dust, pollen, pet fur, and foods. Regular doses of antihistamine can help reduce symptoms. Seek medical advice.

Understanding anaphylaxis

Also known as anaphylactic shock, anaphylaxis is an extreme and severe allergic reaction that affects the entire body. The reaction between the allergic antibody (IgE) and the allergen triggers the sudden release of body chemicals, including histamine, from cells in the blood and tissues. These chemicals act on blood vessels, causing swelling anywhere in the body, especially the lungs, which results in breathing difficulties. Blood pressure falls and the circulatory system can fail, leading to shock.

- **Adrenaline.** A drug called adrenaline (also known as epinephrine) can reverse the effects of anaphylaxis if given quickly, constricting the blood vessels, relaxing the smooth muscles in the lungs, improving breathing, stimulating the heartbeat, and reducing the swelling.

- **Autoinjector.** Anyone who is susceptible to having a severe allergic reaction should carry an autoinjector (EpiPen)—a preloaded syringe containing adrenaline. There are different types and the person will normally know how to use it. If the patient is unable to deliver the medication, follow the instructions on the autoinjector.

MILD ALLERGY

1. **Assess patient.** Ask the patient about any known allergy. Ask if medication, such as an asthma inhaler, is normally carried.

2. **Remove the trigger.** If possible, remove the patient from the trigger—for example take her inside if she is allergic to pollen or remove a bee stinger immediately.

3. **Treat symptoms.** Let her take her normal medication if she has any. Seek medical advice if you are in any doubt about her condition.

4. **If the patient becomes pale and weak, treat for shock (see page 107).** Help her to lie down and raise and support her legs.

SEVERE ALLERGIC REACTION

1. **Call for help.** Call for emergency help immediately, telling the 911 operator that the patient is suffering from a severe allergic reaction and the cause if known. If there is a bee stinger, remove it immediately.

2. **Give medication.** Find the patient's EpiPen (adrenaline—epinephrine—autoinjector) and give it to him. If he cannot use it, you can help him. Hold it with your fist, remove the gray safety cap, and press the end firmly against the thigh. The medication can be given through clothing. Rub the area.

3. **Make patient comfortable.** Help the patient to sit down in whatever position he finds most comfortable for breathing. The best position is sitting upright with his back straight. Do not lie him down. His condition should start to improve.

4. **Monitor patient.** Check his level of consciousness, breathing, and pulse while waiting for emergency help. Note any change and tell emergency services. If he starts to deteriorate, treat as for shock. Lay him down with his head low and raise and support his legs.

5. **Repeat medication.** If his symptoms return, give adrenaline (epinephrine) again every five minutes, until medical help arrives.

MANAGING SERIOUS ALLERGY

- **Always carry medication.** Anyone susceptible to severe allergic reactions will be prescribed a pre-loaded adrenaline injection kit.

- **Carry medical ID.** Wear an ID tag or bracelet and, if possible, carry a card.

- **Avoid known triggers.** Common allergens include foods, such as peanuts, tree nuts (almonds, walnuts, cashews, Brazils), sesame seeds or oil, fish, shellfish, dairy products, and eggs. Non-food causes include wasp or bee stings, latex, penicillin, and other drugs.

ASTHMA ATTACK

When a person has an asthma attack, the air passages narrow and the muscles tighten, making breathing difficult. In addition the mucus that lines the airway becomes sticky. The patient will need prompt help to use her inhaler.

SIGNS OF ASTHMA

- Difficulty breathing, especially breathing out

- Wheezing and coughing

- Difficulty talking

- Blueness around lips and earlobes as condition worsens

GET HELP

If this is a first asthma attack, or the patient does not have an inhaler, call for emergency help immediately.

1. **Give inhaler.** Help the patient find her reliever inhaler and help her to take a puff from it. Tell her to breathe slowly and deeply while she does this. Make sure the patient is using the reliever inhaler and not the preventer inhaler, as this will not help during the attack.

2. **Sit patient down.** Help her to sit down in whatever position she finds most comfortable for breathing. The best position is leaning forward slightly with her back straight. Do not let her lie down. If the attack

does not improve after a few minutes, give her another puff from the inhaler.

3. **Call for help.** If breathing does not improve, the patient's condition becomes worse, or she finds it difficult to talk because of her breathlessness and/or she is becoming exhausted, call for emergency help.

4. **Monitor patient.** Help the patient use her inhaler as necessary and monitor her level of consciousness, breathing, and pulse while you are waiting for help. Make a note of any change in her condition.

5. **If the attack worsens and the patient becomes unconscious, open the airway and check breathing (see page 80).** Be prepared to begin CPR (see page 83).

CHOKING

If a small object "goes down the wrong way," it can block the airway and cause muscle spasm. Young children are also apt to put small objects in their mouths. This can be life-threatening as the air passages that lead to the lungs become partially or totally blocked. Elderly people who are infirm need special attention at mealtimes. Make sure that they are seated, give them small spoonfuls of food, and check that their mouth is completely clear when the meal is finished.

If the patient can still cough, do not intervene, as there is a risk that the obstruction could get into the lungs. There may be another cause for the cough so ask the patient if choking is the reason. Look out for the following symptoms of breathing difficulty:

- Patient suddenly starts coughing, gasping for breath, and has difficulty talking.

- Skin becomes gray-blue (known as cyanosis). This is especially noticeable at the ears, lips, inside the mouth, and fingertips.

- Adult and child (aged 1 to puberty): If the airway is partially blocked, the patient will be able to speak, cough, and breathe. If the airway is completely blocked, the patient will not be able to talk, cough, or breathe.

- Baby (0–12 months): If the airway is partially blocked, the baby can cough but will find it difficult to cry or even to make a noise. If the airway is completely blocked, the baby will not make a sound and will stop breathing.

ADULT/CHILD

1. **Clear a partially obstructed airway.** Tell her to cough and clear an obstruction herself if she can.

2. **Give back blows.** If the airway is completely blocked, help her to bend forward and support her upper body. Give five sharp back blows between the shoulder blades with the heel of your hand, then check her mouth.

3. **Give abdominal thrusts.** If she is still choking, place your arms around her body, with one fist against the abdomen. Grasp the fist with your other hand and pull inward and upward up to five times. Check her mouth again.

4. **Check the person's mouth after every set of back slaps and abdominal thrusts or chest thrusts.** Pick out anything obvious. Don't sweep a finger around the mouth to look for an object, as you may push it farther down the throat or damage the tissues.

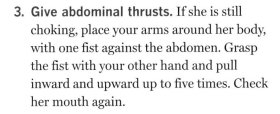

SAFETY FIRST WITH YOUNG CHILDREN
Keep toys with small pieces out of reach of very young children—check the label for suitability.

- Do not give a young child small, hard, or chewy sweets or nuts.
- Stay with your child while he is eating.
- Make sure your child is sitting down whenever he is eating and/or drinking.
- Purée or mash food for a baby until he learns to chew properly.
- When a young child starts wanting to feed himself, give him soft or well-cooked foods to eat.
- Remove fruit seeds.
- Do not leave a baby alone with his bottle or drink.

5. **Get emergency help.** If necessary, repeat steps 2 and 3 up to three times. If the obstruction has not been cleared, call emergency services. Continue with the back blows and abdominal thrusts until help arrives or the patient loses consciousness. Note: Anyone who has been given abdominal thrusts or chest thrusts must be seen by a doctor.

BABY

1. **Give back blows.** If a baby cannot breathe, lay her facedown along your forearm, supporting her head. Using the heel of one hand, give her five sharp blows between her shoulder blades.

2. **Check mouth.** Turn the baby over onto your other arm. Cradle her head in your hand and keep it as low as possible. Look inside her mouth. If the mouth is not clear, go to step 3.

3. **Give chest thrusts.** Keeping the baby along your forearm, support your arm along or across your thigh. Place two fingers a finger's breadth below the nipple line and press sharply inward and upward up to five times.

4. **Get emergency help.** Repeat steps 1 to 3 up to three times. If the mouth is still not clear, take the baby with you and call emergency services. Continue back blows and chest thrusts until help arrives. If the baby loses consciousness, prepare to give CPR.

CARDIOPULMONARY RESUSCITATION (CPR)

If a person is not breathing, his heartbeat will stop. Do CPR (chest compressions and rescue breaths) to help circulation and get oxygen into the body. Early use of a machine called an AED (automated external defibrillator—see page 86) can restart a heart with an abnormal rhythm.

- Open the airway and check breathing. Do not begin CPR if a patient is breathing normally.

- Get help. If you are not alone, send someone to call for help as soon as you have checked breathing. Ask the person to come back and confirm that the call has been made.

- DO NOT press on the ribs, the lower tip of the breastbone, or the upper abdomen when giving chest compressions to a patient.

- If the chest does not rise and fall with a rescue breath, adjust the head position and try again. DO NOT try more than twice before.

Continue giving CPR until emergency help arrives, the patient starts to breathe normally, or you are too tired to keep going. If normal breathing begins at any point, place him in the Recovery Position (see page 114) and await help.

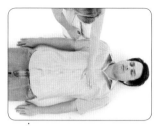

1. **Position your hand.** Make sure the patient is lying on his back on a firm surface. Kneel beside him and place the heel of your hand on the center of the chest.

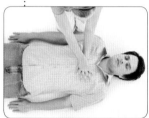

2. **Interlock fingers.** Keeping your arms straight, cover the first hand with the heel of your other hand and interlock the fingers of both hands together. Keep your fingers raised so they do not touch the patient's chest or rib cage.

3. **Give chest compressions.** Lean forward so that your shoulders are directly over the patient's chest and press straight down on the chest about 2 inches. Release the pressure, but not your hands and let the chest come back up. Repeat to give 30 compressions at a rate of 100 compressions per minute.

4. **Open the airway.** Move to the patient's head. Tilt his head and lift his chin to open the airway again. Let his mouth fall open slightly.

5. **Give rescue breaths.** Pinch the nostrils closed with the hand that was on the forehead and support the patient's chin with your other hand. Take a normal breath, put your mouth over the patient's, and blow until you can see his chest rise.

6. **Watch chest fall.** Remove your mouth from the patient's and look along the chest, watching the chest fall. Repeat steps 5 and 6 once.

7. **Repeat chest compressions and rescue breaths.** Place your hands on the chest again and repeat the cycle of 30 chest compressions, followed by two rescue breaths. Continue the cycle.

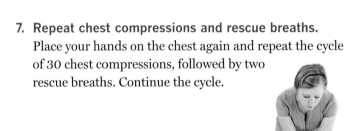

USING AN AUTOMATED EXTERNAL DEFIBRILLATOR (AED)

Give CPR while you wait for the AED. If there is no one available trained in its use, follow the machine's instructions.

- **Attach pads.** Switch on AED. Position pads against the skin as shown on the pack.

- **Listen to machine prompts.** Stand away from the patient and make sure that no one is touching him while the AED is analyzing. It will tell you whether or not a shock is advised.

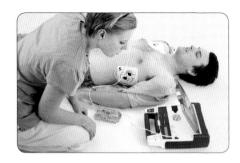

- **If shock advised:** Make sure no one is touching the patient and stand clear. Press the shock button; the patient will "jump." Continue CPR for two more minutes, then the AED will reanalyze the patient. Follow instructions. Leave pads attached if patient recovers.

- **If no shock advised:** Continue CPR for two more minutes, then the AED will reanalyze the patient. Leave pads attached and keep following the AED's instructions, going on to repeat chest compressions.

DIABETIC EMERGENCY

 A diabetic can develop hyperglycemia (raised blood sugar) or hypoglycemia (low blood sugar). Giving sugar will be life-saving if blood sugar is low, and is unlikely to do harm if sugar levels are raised. Diabetics usually know how to control their condition, but even long-term diabetics may be susceptible to an attack.

Suspect low blood sugar if a patient is known to have diabetes and has missed a meal or has recently taken a lot of exercise. Some or all of the following symptoms may be present:

RAISED BLOOD SUGAR (HYPERGLYCEMIA)

This is more likely to develop over several days or even weeks and the symptoms may include:

- Extreme thirst

- Frequent urination, especially at night

- Weight loss

- Itchy skin

- Wounds that heal more slowly than usual

- In the later stages, the patient will become very drowsy, which will lead to unconsciousness—this is an emergency.

Understanding diabetes

Diabetes is a condition in which the body cannot control the level of glucose (sugar) in the blood. Insulin helps to remove glucose from the blood so it can be converted into energy. Diabetes develops either because an organ called the pancreas does not produce insulin (Type 1 diabetes), or because the body's cells are unable to use it (Type 2 diabetes). The condition can result in raised blood sugar levels (hyperglycemia) or low blood sugar (hypoglycemia), both of which are serious.

- **Type 1 diabetes.** This is a lifelong condition that usually begins in childhood or early adulthood. People with Type 1 diabetes need to have insulin every day, normally via a syringe, pump, or an insulin pen.

- **Type 2 diabetes.** This is the most common type. It is associated with obesity, and is more common in the over 40s but can develop in much younger people. Type 2 diabetes is controlled by monitoring a person's diet, controlling weight, and exercising. Oral tablet medication is often needed and some people also need insulin.

LOW BLOOD SUGAR (HYPOGLYCEMIA)

This can occur if the blood sugar–insulin balance is incorrect. A person with diabetes often recognizes the warning signs:

- Feels shaky and weak

- Skin is pale and feels cold and clammy

- Confused, irritable, and behaving irrationally

- Rapid, but full and bounding pulse; patient may tell you that his heart is pounding

- Patient will quickly lose consciousness if he is not given some sugar

If you know that a patient has diabetes and he fails to respond to sugar or his condition begins to deteriorate, call for medical help immediately. A person who has recently been diagnosed with diabetes is more susceptible to a "hypo" attack, especially while he is becoming used to balancing his sugar–insulin levels.

HYPERGLYCEMIA

1. **Call emergency help.** If a patient collapses and you suspect hyperglycemia, open the airway and check breathing. Call for emergency help.

2. **Monitor patient.** If he is breathing place him in the recovery position (see page 114). Check and note his level of consciousness, breathing, and pulse.

3. **Recheck patient.** Continue to recheck the patient regularly while you are waiting for medical help to arrive.

HYPOGLYCEMIA

1. **Sit patient down.** Reassure the patient and help him to sit down on a chair or on the floor if he is feeling faint.

2. **Give sugar.** Provided the patient is fully conscious and alert, give him a sugary drink, such as fruit juice, or some glucose tablets. People who have diabetes often carry a dose of glucose concentrate or have some sugary food in their pocket as a precaution.

3. **Check response.** If the patient improves quickly after eating or drinking something, follow this with some slower-release carbohydrate food, such as a cereal bar, a sandwich, piece of fruit, biscuits and milk, or the next meal, if it is due.

4. **Find medication.** Help the patient to find his glucose testing kit and medication and let him check his glucose levels and take his insulin if required. Stay with him until he recovers completely. It is important to seek medical advice if you are at all concerned about the patient.

HYPOTHERMIA AND FROSTBITE

When the core body temperature falls below 95°F, the body shuts down the blood supply to the surface blood vessels to keep vital organs such as the heart supplied with blood. This leads to a condition known as hypothermia.

Symptoms and signs of hypothermia are the same whatever the cause or age of the patient. You may also see signs of frostbite on the patient's fingers and toes.

- Skin—feels cold and dry, and looks pale

- Lacks energy

- Shivering in the early stages—this is the body's way of creating heat

AS HYPOTHERMIA DEEPENS

- Patient becomes disoriented and starts to behave irrationally; she will become more lethargic and may no longer be fully conscious and alert.

- Eventually the patient will lose consciousness.

- Breaths become very slow and shallow.

- Pulse slows down and gets gradually weaker and irregular; if the patient is not warmed up, the heart stops.

1. **Warm up gradually.** Only start to warm someone up if there is no risk of her becoming cold again. If you are inside, start to warm the room, or move to a warmer room. Remove any wet clothes. Wrap her up in several layers of blankets to trap heat. Put a hat on her head.

2. **Warning.** Do not warm a patient with direct heat, such as a hot-water bottle, or put her beside an electric fire. Do not give her alcohol, as this dilates the blood vessels, decreasing the body's ability to retain heat. Do not rub or massage the person as, in severe hypothermia, there is a risk of heart attack. If a patient becomes unconscious, open the airway and check breathing. Be prepared to begin CPR (see page 83).

3. **Give warm drink and food.** Provided the patient is fully conscious, give her a warm (not hot) drink and a high-energy food such as chocolate for fast energy. You may need to help her.

4. **A healthy adult or older child** can be warmed up in a bath if he can climb in and out unaided and there is no risk of him becoming cold again. Note: Do not warm up an elderly person in a bath, as this may send cold blood to the heart or brain too suddenly, and may cause a stroke or heart attack.

5. **Get emergency help.** Call emergency services as soon as possible. Check and make a note of her level of consciousness, breathing, and pulse regularly until help arrives.

Treating a baby

Young babies have very under-developed temperature control mechanisms, so can become hypothermic relatively quickly in a cold room. A baby will become very floppy, but may have bright pink skin. Her skin will feel very cold. She will not want to eat or drink.

WARM UP GRADUALLY. Either warm the room or take the baby into a warmer room. Wrap the baby in warm blankets. Keep her head covered with a hat or the blanket, but leave her face exposed. Cuddle her so that you are using your own body heat for warmth.

GET HELP. Either call emergency services or take the baby to the hospital if you can keep her warm. Check level of consciousness, breathing, and pulse.

FROSTBITE

The extremities, usually the fingers and toes, can literally freeze if exposed to severe cold. Tissues can be permanently damaged if treatment is not given quickly.

- Patient may have pins and needles in affected areas; later he may have no feeling

- Skin may be waxy and pale and feel cold and hard

- Skin may turn from white to mottled blue/gray

1. **Stop and find shelter.** Get the patient into a shelter. Do not warm the affected area unless there is no risk of refreezing. Do not remove her gloves or shoes if she is likely to have to walk any farther.

2. **Warm up gradually.** Tell the patient to put her hands in her armpits to warm them up gently using her own body warmth. She can put her feet in your armpits to warm them up.

3. **Place affected parts in warm water.** Once you are inside, remove the patient's gloves or shoes and place her hands or feet in warm water. Try to remove rings or jewelry (do not force this though). Dry the affected area and wrap it in a loose, dry, non-fluffy bandage.

4. **Get medical help.** The patient should be taken to the hospital. If she is in pain, she can take the recommended dose of her normal pain relief tablet, such as acetaminophen or ibuprofen.

As the skin is warmed up, it may become bright red, feel hot, and be very painful. If the tissues are damaged, the affected area may turn black because of a lack of blood supply to the area.

POTENTIAL HEART ATTACK

A heart attack is caused by an obstruction of the blood supply to the heart muscle (usually by a blood clot in the coronary blood vessels). The outcome depends on how much of the muscle is affected and how quickly help can be given. If you think someone is having a heart attack, always call for help rather than waiting to see if the symptoms subside. A patient is three times more likely to survive if he receives advanced medical help within an hour of having a heart attack.

These are the common signs and symptoms of a heart attack. A patient will experience some, but not necessarily all. If the pain subsides with rest, it could be angina (see page 95).

- Suddenly feels faint or dizzy

- Severe chest pain—persistent and vice-like, spreading up to the jaw and down one or both arms—which does not subside when the patient rests

- Discomfort high in abdomen—may feel like severe indigestion

- Breathlessness—patient may be gasping for air

ADDITIONAL SYMPTOMS

- Fear—feels sense of impending doom

- Pale, gray (ashen), clammy, or sweaty skin

- Nausea and vomiting

- Rapid, weak, and irregular pulse

- Collapses—often without warning

- Possible loss of consciousness

A CONSCIOUS PATIENT

1. **Ease strain on heart.** Make the patient as comfortable as possible, in a half-sitting position, with his head and shoulders well supported and knees bent to ease strain on the heart. Loosen clothing at the neck, chest, and waist.

2. **Call for emergency help.** Keep bystanders away from the patient.

3. **Give angina medication.** If the patient has medication for angina (see opposite) help him to take it. Keep him calm and encourage him to rest.

4. **Give aspirin.** If the patient is fully conscious, give him a full-dose (300mg) aspirin tablet. Tell him to chew it slowly so that it dissolves and is absorbed into the bloodstream more quickly when it reaches the stomach. Aspirin helps to break down blood clots, minimizing muscle damage.

5. **Monitor patient.** Regularly check and make a note of consciousness, breathing, and pulse.

AN UNCONSCIOUS PATIENT

1. **Open airway.** Check for breathing and be prepared to begin CPR (see page 83), as the heart may stop.

2. **Send for AED.** Ask someone to bring an AED (automated external defibrillator—see page 86), if possible, while you treat the patient. AEDs can deliver a shock to correct an abnormal heart rhythm called ventricular fibrillation—the cause of some heart attacks. The machines are found in most public places—shopping centers and train stations, for example.

3. **Operate AED.** An AED is simple to use. Attach the pads as indicated on the machine; then the machine will talk the operator through the process. An AED will only deliver a

shock if the patient's condition indicates that it is necessary. If you have attached an AED to a patient, leave the machine switched on at all times and leave the pads attached, even if the patient recovers.

WHAT NEXT?

- Wait for the emergency medical technicians. The earlier a person receives advanced medical help, the greater the chances of survival.

- Diagnosis will be confirmed at the hospital with an electrocardiogram (ECG) and blood tests. Advanced care may include a stay in the intensive care unit and treatment with drugs or even surgery. The aim is to minimize pain, restore the blood supply to the damaged heart muscle, and prevent complications.

- Hospital treatment for a heart attack will be followed by a period of rehabilitation.

ANGINA

If the pain subsides after the person rests for a few minutes, it is likely that it is an angina attack. This is a long-term condition in which the coronary (heart) arteries are narrowed, so that the heart muscle cannot get enough blood to meet its demands. Someone diagnosed with angina will have been given medication for use in an attack.

- **Reassure.** Keep the patient calm; sit her down.

- **Assist with medication.** Help the patient find her medication—usually a tablet or spray. If necessary, help her take it. If a patient has no medication at hand, call for emergency help immediately. Treat as described above.

- **Keep watch.** The attack should ease within a few minutes. If the pain does not ease or the person has no medication, treat as a heart attack.

SUDDEN VISION PROBLEMS

 Vision problems can develop following an injury to the eye or head. They can also result from disorders of the nervous system or of the eyes. Age-related deterioration is the most likely cause of vision problems and these can develop gradually or suddenly. Any sudden change should be investigated, as early treatment can prevent permanent loss of sight. If a patient experiences problems with his vision after a blow to the head, or if a patient (adult or child) complains of sudden loss of sight in one or both eyes, call for medical assistance without delay.

As well as a reduction of vision, a person may experience the following symptoms:

- Sudden blurred or distorted vision

- Pain in and around one or both eyes

- Redness and watering

ADDITIONAL SYMPTOMS

- Difficulty focusing or colors may appear faded

- Burning or gritty sensation in the eyes

- Sudden appearance of "floaters" in the eye—these are spots that appear to be "on" the eye

- Partial loss of field of vision

- Obvious eye injury

SYMPTOM FINDER

SYMPTOMS	POSSIBLE CAUSES
Red itchy eyes, with yellow pus-like discharge	If vision is restored when the discharge is cleaned away, it may be conjunctivitis, an infection of the conjunctiva (the membrane that covers the eyes). Seek medical advice as treatment may be needed.
Sudden onset of double vision	Bleeding into the brain after a stroke or head injury, or it could be a symptom of a disorder of the nervous system. Call for emergency help.
Flashing lights and spots in front of the eyes	If this precedes a headache, it could be a migraine. If it occurs with no warning, it could be a detached retina at the back of the eye. Call for emergency help.
Blurred or double vision	Vision can be affected by diabetes-related disorders, some prescription drugs, ingestion of poisons, and clouding of the eye lens (cataracts). Seek medical advice or take the patient to hospital if severe.
Blurred or distorted vision with pain in one or both eyes	Glaucoma, a condition caused by excess fluid in the eye that results in a buildup of pressure in the eyeball. Seek medical advice.

1. **Reassure patient.** The patient is likely to be very frightened if there is loss of vision.

2. **Treat any injury.** If the eye is injured, help her to lie down and support her head. Give her a pad to hold over the injured eye. If the patient has splashed chemicals in her eye, see page 129.

3. **Seek medical advice.** Advise the patient to call her doctor, or make the call for her. If you are in any doubt about her condition, take her to the hospital or call 911.

DETACHED RETINA

The retina is the innermost layer at the back of the eye. It contains millions of light receptors that convert the image formed by the eye's optical system into impulses that are carried along the optic nerve to the brain. The retina can become detached from its underlying layer and may be torn. This causes sudden full or partial loss of vision, rather like a curtain falling over part of the eye. Take patient to the hospital. This is a serious condition that can lead to blindness if it is not diagnosed and treated very quickly. The tear can be repaired surgically, which can restore vision and prevent further deterioration.

SNOW BLINDNESS

The surface of the eyes can be damaged by over-exposure to ultraviolet (UV) light. This can be caused by the glare of sunlight on snow, concrete, or water and can be prevented by wearing UV-protecting sunglasses.

1. **Assess symptoms.** The patient will experience a gritty feeling and excruciating pain in the eye. His eyes may be red and watering.

2. **Take patient to the hospital.** Give him clean pads to hold against his eyes if there is likely to be any delay.

3. **Rest the eyes.** The patient will be advised to wear sunglasses and stay out of the sun until his eyes have healed.

SUDDEN HEARING LOSS

Most hearing loss is gradual and age-related but a number of conditions can result in sudden loss of hearing over a matter of days or even hours. In many cases, the cause is an ear infection or wax blockage that can be treated easily. Consult a doctor or hospital if sudden hearing loss occurs without an obvious cause in one or both ears.

CAUSES OF TEMPORARY HEARING PROBLEMS

- Blocked nose as a result of a severe cold or hay fever—this can cause a buildup of mucus against the eardrum, especially in children.

- Pressure change during takeoff and landing when flying.

- Brief exposure to loud noise, such as music, which can leave a loud ringing in the ears for a few hours. A sudden, very loud noise such as an explosion can damage the eardrum.

- Infection of the outer or inner ear.

- Buildup of wax in the ear canals.

- Ménière's disease—a serious disorder in which excess fluid collects in the inner ear, resulting in severe dizziness.

- Head injury—if sudden hearing loss follows a blow to the head, call for emergency help immediately.

1. **Reassure patient.** If the deafness results from a change in pressure after flying, tell the patient to hold his nose and blow through his nose until he feels his ears "pop." If he has a cold or hay fever, hearing will return when he recovers. Ringing in the ears after exposure to loud noise should stop in a few hours.

2. **Seek medical advice.** Arrange for the patient to see his doctor for any other cause. If he cannot contact his doctor, take him to the hospital.

3. **Treat earache.** If the patient is in pain, suggest he takes a dose of acetaminophen medication. Give him a hot-water bottle wrapped in a towel to hold against the ear to help soothe the pain.

The patient's doctor may prescribe a course of antibiotics as treatment for an ear infection or burst eardrum. The doctor will arrange a follow-up appointment to check that the infection has responded. A burst eardrum will normally heal by itself. If the cause cannot be identified, a patient will be referred to a specialist for tests to assess the cause and measure the degree of hearing loss.

PROTECTING HEARING

Persistent exposure to loud noise can cause permanent hearing loss, but there are steps that can be taken to prevent damage to ears.

- Wear ear protection. Wear ear plugs or ear defenders if exposed to sustained loud noises at work and get hearing checked regularly.

- Keep sound levels low. Make sure the sound level of headphones is low enough to be able to hear a conversation above them.

- Limit listening time. Restrict listening to personal stereo systems to about an hour at a time.

SUSPECTED MISCARRIAGE

A miscarriage is the loss of a fetus at any time during the first 23 weeks of pregnancy, but most happen during the first 12 weeks. As a miscarriage can happen without warning, and may result in serious blood loss, treat it as an emergency. The loss of a pregnancy can have a serious emotional impact, so the woman will need reassurance and support.

Miscarriage is very common, especially in the first 12 weeks of pregnancy. Symptoms may be similar to a normal menstrual period.

- Vaginal bleeding—occasionally severe

- Abdominal pain and low backache—similar to period pain

- Possible severe cramping pains—similar to labor pains

Additional symptoms:
- In some cases, bleeding may be slight and develop over a few days

- Blood clots may be passed

- If blood loss is severe or has been prolonged, symptoms of shock may be evident

- The patient may say she has passed some tissue during the bleeding

- The patient may become very distressed

1. **Reassure the woman.** If you suspect that a pregnant woman is having a miscarriage, arrange for some privacy. Help her to lie down in a comfortable position. Make sure she has a sanitary napkin, or a small, clean towel, if she

needs one. Do not give her a tampon. Assess the level of bleeding.

2. **Call for help.** If bleeding is slight, advise her to call her doctor or midwife. If bleeding is severe, call emergency services or take her to the hospital.

3. **Monitor the patient.** Check and make a note of her level of consciousness, breathing, and pulse. Check regularly until medical help arrives. If the woman becomes very weak and/or collapses, treat as for shock. Raise and support her legs and cover her with a blanket to keep her warm.

TAKE CARE

- Preserve any tissue that a woman passes and give it to the medical team attending her.

- All bleeding in pregnancy should be assessed by a midwife and/or doctor. Bleeding during pregnancy does not necessarily mean the woman is having a miscarriage. Occasional light bleeding in the first 12 weeks of pregnancy is not uncommon; many women go on to have a healthy pregnancy.

- If a newly pregnant woman complains of very severe abdominal pain, particularly if it is one-sided, call 911 or take her straight to the hospital. This could be an ectopic pregnancy (when the fetus is developing outside the womb), which is a medical emergency.

SEIZURES

A seizure is caused by a burst of excess electrical activity in the brain, which results in a brief disruption in the messages that pass between brain cells. Seizures can result from epilepsy, but in young children they can be triggered by a fever. If a seizure lasts five minutes or more, or a patient has a series of seizures without regaining consciousness, get help. This is a medical emergency.

Seizures range from brief absences to episodes of convulsing and losing consciousness. The pattern is similar whatever the trigger.

FEBRILE SEIZURE IN YOUNG CHILD

A young child's temperature control system is not fully developed. Fever can trigger a febrile seizure. If a child has had a febrile seizure, she is likely to have another one if she has a fever again; this does not mean she will develop epilepsy.

- Child has a raised temperature

- Collapse followed by seizure

- History of febrile seizures with previous illness

1. **Protect child.** Do not restrain the child, place padding such as pillows around her to prevent her injuring herself, for example, from falling off the bed.

2. **Cool the child.** Seizures result from a raised body temperature. Cool the child by removing the bedclothes. Remove clothing, though you may have to wait for convulsive movements to stop before you can do this. Open a window if possible but do not let the child get too cold.

3. **Call for medical help.** Place the child in the recovery position (see page 114) when the seizure stops. Check

and note the level of consciousness, breathing, and pulse. Re-check regularly until medical help arrives.

Do not cool a child by sponging with water. This can make surface blood vessels contract and conserve body heat, causing temperature to rise.

MAJOR SEIZURE

Symptoms typically follow this pattern:

- Sudden collapse

- Patient becomes rigid and may arch her back

- Convulsive movements begin—these may affect one or both sides of the body

- Breathing becomes difficult—patient may clench her jaw. Blood or blood-stained saliva may appear at the mouth (she has probably bitten her lips or tongue). Do not be tempted to put anything in her mouth. There may also be signs of lost bowel or bladder control.

- Eventually, the muscles relax and breathing returns to normal.

- Patient will wake up, but may be dazed.

- Patient is likely to fall into a deep sleep, after which she may not be aware of anything that has happened.

If a person is having a seizure do not restrain her or attempt to "bring her around." Do not try to put anything in the person's mouth during the seizure. Stay calm, do not frighten her by making abrupt movements or shouting. Assume the patient is unaware of what is happening, or what has happened.

1. **Clear a space.** Try to break the patient's fall. Remove any objects or furniture from around the patient, or place padding against her so that she cannot injure herself.

2. **Protect the patient's head.** Place cushions or rolled towels or blankets around the patient's head to protect her further.

3. **Check for epilepsy information.** Once the convulsive movements have stopped, check the patient's arms, neck, or pockets, as she may be wearing a medical ID bracelet or necklace or have a card that describes her condition and normal seizure pattern.

4. **Place in recovery position.** If she falls asleep, open the airway and check breathing. Make a note of how long the convulsions lasted.

5. **Monitor the patient.** Check and make a note of her level of consciousness, breathing and pulse and recheck regularly. Stay with her until she wakes up. Do not give her anything to eat or drink until she has fully recovered.

WHEN TO CALL EMERGENCY SERVICES

- You know that it is the patient's first seizure.

- The seizure continues for longer than five minutes.

- She remains unconscious for longer than 10 minutes after the convulsions.

- One seizure follows another without her regaining consciousness in between.

- The person is injured during the seizure.

- You are concerned about the patient's condition and believe that she needs urgent medical attention.

ABSENCE SEIZURE

In an absence seizure, the person may appear to be daydreaming or switching off. She will be briefly unconscious and totally unaware of what is happening around her.
There may be unexplained actions, such as lip smacking or rubbing hands.

1. **Help patient to safety.** Sit the patient down somewhere quiet. Make sure she cannot hurt herself, for example by walking into a road. If she is inside, clear a space around her.

2. **Check for epilepsy information.** The patient may be carrying a card or wearing a bracelet that describes her condition.

3. **Reassure patient.** Stay with the patient until you are certain that she has fully recovered—be aware that an absence seizure can be followed by a major seizure. Calmly reassure her and explain anything that she has missed.

SHOCK

Medical shock is a life-threatening condition that develops if the circulatory system fails to provide sufficient oxygen-rich blood to the heart and brain. Severe bleeding is the most common cause, but it can also follow fluid loss from burns, vomiting, or diarrhea or be the result of an allergic reaction or heart failure.

Signs of shock worsen as the circulatory system fails. Suspect shock after, for example, severe bleeding (see page 173), but also if any of the following occur with no obvious wound:

- Rapid pulse at first, which becomes weaker. By the time half the blood is lost from the circulatory system (about three liters in an adult), you may not be able to feel the pulse at the wrist.

- Profuse sweating with cold, clammy skin.

- Fast, but shallow, breathing.

- Cyanosis (blue-gray skin) at the ears, lips, inside the mouth, and at the fingertips. If you press a fingernail and then let go, the healthy pink color will not return quickly.

- Patient will become weak and feel dizzy. He may feel nauseous and may even be sick.

- Patient will begin to feel very thirsty.

- As the oxygen to the brain reduces, the patient will feel restless and may be aggressive. He will be yawning and gasping for air. Eventually he will become unconscious and his heart may stop.

SIGNS OF INTERNAL BLEEDING

- Signs of shock (see above) but no obvious injury

- Bruising on the skin that matches the pattern of clothes and worsens as the area swells

- Patient may tell you that the abdomen or chest feels swollen, as if there is extra fluid inside

- Bleeding from body openings (see below)

- Sudden collapse and loss of consciousness some time after an injury

- Information from the patient or a bystander that indicates possible internal injury

If you suspect shock, call emergency services or ask someone else to make the call while you look after the patient, following the steps below. Shock is life-threatening—suspect it if you notice any of the symptoms or signs even if there is no obvious injury.

1. **Treat obvious cause.** Treat severe bleeding by applying direct pressure to the wound (see page 172). Cool any burns (see page 126). Raise and support the injury.

BLEEDING FROM BODY OPENINGS

BODY OPENING	APPEARANCE AND POSSIBLE CAUSES
Ears/Nose	Bright red blood in the ear is likely to be caused by injury to the outer part of the ear or eardrum. Bright red blood from the nose results from a ruptured blood vessel in the nose. The watery blood that appears after a head injury is fluid from around the brain mixed with blood from the ear and nose.
Mouth	Coughed-up bright red, frothy blood indicates bleeding in the lungs. Dark-reddish blood that looks like coffee grounds comes from the digestive system.
Anus	Fresh bright red blood comes from the lower part of the intestine or bowel. Darker, tar-like stools indicate injury farther up the digestive system.
Urethra	Reddish urine, with possible clots, indicates possible bleeding from the kidneys, ureters, bladder, or urethra.
Vagina	Fresh or dark-red blood could be a sign of menstruation, but it could also be caused by infection, a miscarriage, childbirth, or sexual assault.

2. **Lie patient down.** Reassure the patient and tell him not to move unnecessarily. Help him to lie down on a rug or blanket. Do not put anything under his head, leave it low. Raise and support his legs as high as you can above his heart; for example, rest his feet on a chair. If the patient has a suspected broken leg, do not raise the affected leg, but raise the other leg, if possible.

3. **Loosen clothing.** Loosen any tight clothing, especially around his neck, chest, and waist, that could restrict blood circulation around the body.

4. **Keep the patient warm.** Cover him with a blanket or coats. Do not warm him with a hot-water bottle or electric blanket. The aim of treatment is to keep vital organs supplied with blood. If you put a hot-water bottle on the patient's skin, blood will be drawn to the surface of the body and away from the center where it is needed.

5. **Call emergency help.** Call 911. Tell the dispatcher that you suspect shock, and give as much information as you can about the possible cause.

6. **Monitor patient.** Check and note the level of consciousness, breathing, and pulse. Recheck regularly until medical help arrives. If the patient is thirsty, moisten his lips with a clean damp cloth. Do not give the patient anything to eat or drink, as he may need an anesthetic at the hospital. If the patient loses consciousness, open the airway and check his breathing. Be prepared to begin CPR.

STROKE

Also known as a brain attack, a stroke occurs when the blood supply to part of the brain is cut off or reduced because of a ruptured blood vessel or a clot in one of the blood vessels that supplies the brain. The effects will depend on the part of the brain that is affected. The sooner a patient receives hospital treatment, the better the chances of recovery.

THE "FAST" TEST

A quick test to help check for the most obvious signs of a stroke, FAST requires an assessment of three specific symptoms. If the patient fails any one of these tests, call for emergency help:

- **F**acial weakness: Can the person smile? Does his mouth or eye droop?

- **A**rm weakness: Can the person raise both of his arms together?

- **S**peech problems: Can the person speak clearly and understand what you say?

- **T**ime to call!

OTHER SIGNS OF A STROKE

- Sudden weakness on one or both sides of the body that affects arms and/or legs

- Difficulty understanding and/or confusion

- Rapid loss of sight or blurred vision

- Sudden severe headache

- Collapse

Tell the emergency services that you have assessed the patient using the FAST test and you suspect a stroke. Do not give anything to eat or drink, as the patient may not be able to swallow and could choke. If the patient becomes unconscious, open the airway and check breathing. Be prepared to begin CPR (see page 83).

1. **Check face.** Look at the patient. Do you notice any facial weakness? Ask her to smile. If she has had a stroke she may only be able to smile on one side. The other side of her face may droop.

2. **Check arms.** Ask the patient if she can lift her arms. If she has had a stroke she may only be able to lift one arm—on the same side of the body that she can smile.

3. **Check speech.** Talk to the patient. Can she understand what you are saying and can she speak clearly? If the patient has had a stroke her speech may be impaired and she may not understand you.

4. **Call for emergency help.** If the answer is yes to any one of these assessments, suspect a stroke. Call for emergency help immediately. Reassure the patient and monitor her breathing and pulse as well as level of consciousness while you are waiting for help.

UNCONSCIOUS ADULT

An unconscious person has no muscle control in his throat, so the tongue can fall back and block the airways, preventing breathing. He cannot cough or swallow so risks choking on fluid or vomit. Fast action can be life-saving. If a person is not breathing, the heart can stop, so begin CPR immediately (see step 4). If the patient is a child or baby, go to page 116, as there are important differences in the way unconsciousness is managed in children.

Find out whether or not an unconscious patient is breathing before you call emergency services, as this is likely to be the first question you will be asked. If you are not alone, send someone to call for help as soon as you have checked breathing. Ask the person to come back and confirm that the call has been made.

1. **Tilt head.** Kneel next to the patient—level with his shoulders—put one hand on his forehead in front of the hairline, then tilt the head back. His mouth will fall slightly open.

2. **Life chin.** Place two fingers of your other hand on the point of the patient's chin, then lift it. This action will lift the

tongue away from the back of the throat, opening the air passage to the lungs.

3. **Check breathing.** Put your ear as near as possible to the patient's mouth and nose and look toward his chest. Listen for breathing sounds, feel for breaths against your face, and look to see if the chest is moving. Do this for up to 10 seconds.

4. **If not breathing.** Call for emergency help. Start cardiopulmonary resuscitation (CPR—see pages 83–86). If you are in a public place, ask someone to fetch an AED machine (see page 86), which may correct the heart rhythm.

5. **If breathing normally.** Check for and treat conditions that affect circulation, such as severe bleeding or burns. Call for emergency help. If possible, place the patient in the recovery position (see next page). Note any change in the patient's condition while you are waiting for help.

THE RECOVERY POSITION

If the patient is breathing normally, place him on his side in the recovery position (unless you suspect serious back injury. In this position his airway is open, fluid and/or vomit can drain, and he cannot roll forward. Try not to leave a patient, but you may need to go and call for help. If you have help, when you place the patient in the recovery position, one person can support his head while you roll him onto his side.

1. **Position arms and legs.** Remove anything bulky from the patient's pockets. Ensure his legs are straight, then kneel beside him, level with chest. Place the arm nearest to you at a right angle to his body with the palm facing upward. Pull his far leg up at the knee until his foot is resting flat on the ground. Lift his other arm, bring it across his body toward you, and hold the back of his hand against his cheek.

2. **Turn the patient.** Grasp his raised knee with one hand and support the hand against his cheek with your other hand. Pull on the knee and gently roll the patient toward you. Keep the patient's head, back, and neck aligned during turning. If you have help, one person can support the patient's head while you roll him onto his side.

3. **Adjust the head position.** Tilt his head back slightly to keep the airway open. The patient's uppermost hand should be under his cheek to help maintain the correct position.

4. **Adjust the leg and arm.** Make sure the patient's upper leg is at a right angle at his hip and knee, his lower leg and back align, and his lower arm is at a right angle at the shoulder and elbow.

5. **Monitor patient.** While you are waiting for help, monitor the patient's level of consciousness, breathing, and pulse and note any changes. If normal breathing stops, begin CPR (see page 83).

UNCONSCIOUS CHILD

Use this sequence to treat a child aged between one year old and puberty. If a child stops breathing, the cause is more likely to be a breathing difficulty than a heart problem, so begin by giving rescue breaths to raise blood oxygen levels. If you have help, ask the person to call emergency services as soon as you know the child is not breathing. If you are on your own and the child is not breathing, carry out CPR for one minute before stopping to make the call for emergency help.

1. **Open airway and check breathing.** Tilt the child's head back and lift the chin. Put your ear next to her mouth: look, listen, and feel for breaths for up to 10 seconds. If she is not breathing, go to step 2. If breathing normally, place the child in the recovery position, as for an adult (see page 114).

2. **Give rescue breaths.** Tilt her head and lift her chin; let the child's mouth fall open slightly. Pick out any visible obstruction from the mouth— do not do a finger sweep. Pinch the nostrils closed, take a breath, put your mouth over the child's, and blow steadily until you see her chest rise. Remove your mouth and watch the chest fall. If the chest

does not rise and fall with a rescue breath, adjust the head position and try again. Give the patient five rescue breaths.

3. **Give chest compressions.** Place the heel of one hand on the center of the chest. With your shoulder directly over your hand, press straight down about one-third of the depth of the chest. Release the pressure, but not your hand; let the chest relax. Give 30 compressions at a rate of 100 compressions per minute. Do not press on the ribs, the lower tip of the breastbone, or the upper abdomen when giving chest compressions.

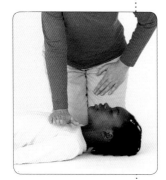

4. **Repeat rescue breaths and compressions.** Tilt the child's head, lift her chin, and repeat rescue breaths—this time give TWO rescue breaths. Continue a cycle of 30 compressions followed by two rescue breaths.

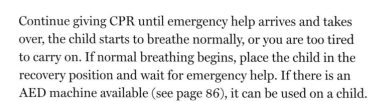

Continue giving CPR until emergency help arrives and takes over, the child starts to breathe normally, or you are too tired to carry on. If normal breathing begins, place the child in the recovery position and wait for emergency help. If there is an AED machine available (see page 86), it can be used on a child.

UNCONSCIOUS BABY

Use this sequence to treat an infant less than one year old. Talk to the baby and tap the foot to assess consciousness; never shake a baby. If a baby's breathing stops, begin by giving rescue breaths. Place the baby on a firm surface before you start. If you have help, ask the person to call emergency services as soon you know the baby is not breathing. If you are on your own and the baby is not breathing, carry out rescue breaths and chest compressions (CPR) for one minute before stopping to make the call for emergency help. Note: An AED cannot be used on an infant aged less than one year old.

1. **Open airway and check breathing.** Tilt the baby's head back and lift the chin. Put your ear next to the baby's mouth: look, listen, and feel for breaths for up to  10 seconds. If she is not breathing, go to the next step. If breathing normally go to step 5.

2. **Give rescue breaths.** Tilt the baby's head slightly and lift the chin. Pick out any visible obstruction from the mouth and nose—do not do a finger sweep. Put your 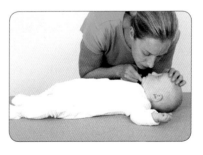 mouth over the baby's mouth and nose and blow steadily until you see the chest rise. Remove your mouth and watch the chest fall. If the chest does not rise and fall with a

rescue breath, adjust the head position and try again. Give five breaths.

3. **Give chest compressions.**
Place two fingers on the center of the chest. With your shoulder over your hand, press straight down about one-third of the depth of the chest. Release the pressure, but not your hand; let the chest relax.
Give 30 compressions at a rate of 100 per minute. Do not press on the ribs, the lower tip of the breastbone, or the upper abdomen when giving chest compressions.

4. **Repeat rescue breaths and compressions.** Tilt the baby's head, lift the chin, and repeat rescue breaths— this time give TWO rescue breaths. Continue a cycle of 30 compressions and two rescue breaths. Continue
giving CPR until emergency help arrives, the baby starts to breathe normally, or you are too tired to carry on. If normal breathing begins, hold the baby in the recovery position (see below) and await emergency help.

5. **If breathing normally.**
Hold the baby with the head lower than the body in the recovery position. Call for emergency help and monitor the level of consciousness, breathing, and pulse while waiting.

CHILDBIRTH

Childbirth is a natural process that can be lengthy, especially with a first baby. It generally happens around the 40th week of pregnancy, but about two weeks either side is normal.

A pregnant woman is likely to be more anxious if labor starts unexpectedly. If a woman goes into labor, find out the expected delivery date and ask if she has her maternity notes—these will have important contact details and medical notes. Offer her reassurance while you wait for emergency services or help to deliver the baby. Ask the woman who else she would like you to call.

About one baby in 10 is born before the 37th week of pregnancy. If it is close to 37 weeks, the birth may proceed as normal, but it is vital to get the mother to a hospital. Some labors start earlier for a number of reasons. If contractions begin well before the baby is due, it may be possible for doctors to stop them with drugs. The mother will also be given steroid injections to help the baby's lungs, so she can breathe properly after the birth.

THE FOLLOWING SIGNS WILL TELL YOU HOW FAR LABOR HAS PROGRESSED

- Possible contractions—these last up to a minute and come at intervals of five to 20 minutes initially, becoming closer as the labor progresses. Note the length of each contraction and the time taken between the beginning of one contraction to the start of the next.

- Rupture of the membrane around the baby can cause fluid to gush out (the waters breaking). Once this happens, there is an increased risk of infection, as the baby's protective layer has gone.

continued on page 122

The stages of labor

Labor has three distinct stages. The first prepares the woman's body for the birth. The baby is born in the second stage. The afterbirth (placenta) is delivered in the third stage.

1. **FIRST STAGE** This stage of labor can last several hours, although it may be shorter in second and later pregnancies. The uterus begins contractions, which help to press the baby's head against the cervix. The cervix gradually opens and "thins" until it is 10cm in diameter. During this stage, a plug of mucus will be expelled. In addition, the water around the baby (amniotic fluid) may gush out.

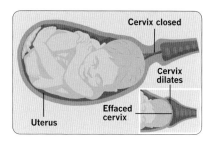

Cervix closed

Cervix dilates

Effaced cervix

Uterus

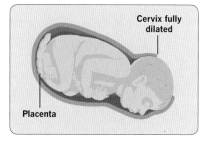

Cervix fully dilated

Placenta

2. **SECOND STAGE** When the cervix is fully dilated (open) the woman's contractions change and she will feel a desire to push the baby out—this is a sign that the baby is about to be born. This stage normally lasts from 10 minutes to an hour, but it can be longer.

3. **THIRD STAGE** Ten minutes to half an hour after the baby is born, the third stage begins. The uterus contracts again. The placenta, known as the afterbirth, comes away from the wall of the uterus and is expelled from the body along with the umbilical cord.

continued from page 120

1. **Call emergency help.** Tell the dispatcher the mother's due date, the place where she was expecting to give birth, and the stage of labor she has reached.

2. **During first stage: Listen to the woman and reassure her.** She may be very worried, especially if the labor is earlier than expected. Help her into a comfortable position and encourage her to breathe slowly and steadily.

3. **Time her contractions.** Make a note of the length and the frequency of her contractions. These will get stronger and more frequent. If she is uncomfortable, she may ask you to massage her back with the heel of your hands. If she is very hot, cool her face and neck with a damp sponge or cloth.

4. **During second stage: If the woman tells you that she wants to push, this is a sign that the second stage has started.** Ask her to remove any clothes that could interfere with the birth. Find a sheet to put underneath her and keep the area clean. Support her, but do not interfere with the birth.

5. **Wrap the baby.** As soon as the baby is born, give her to her mother. Wrap them both in a towel and/or blanket. The baby will be very slippery so handle carefully. Do not cut the cord. Monitor both the mother and baby while you wait for help.

6. **If the umbilical cord is around the baby's neck as she emerges, try to ease it over the head to prevent strangulation.** Do not pull on the cord.

7. **If the baby does not cry or make a sound after being born, do not slap her.** Open the airway and check breathing. Be prepared to begin CPR if she is not breathing (see page 83).

Handling Emergencies

8. **During third stage.** Soon after the birth, contractions will recommence and the mother will deliver the afterbirth. Let this happen naturally (it can take up to 30 minutes). Do not interfere and do not cut the cord. The doctor and midwife will need to check that the afterbirth is complete.

9. **If the bleeding is profuse after the third stage, or the mother is in any pain, keep her warm and lie her down with her legs raised and supported, as there is a risk of shock developing (see page 107).**

PANIC ATTACK

This is a sudden bout of extreme anxiety that can be brought on by a strong fear of something (phobia) or an emotional upset. A panic attack is often accompanied by hyperventilation and/or an abnormally fast heart rate.

SYMPTOMS

- Signs of unnaturally fast breathing, such as hyperventilation or overbreathing

- A very fast pulse rate

- Feeling of tension that causes a headache or chest tightness

- The patient may be very apprehensive and may even have a fear of dying

Do not restrain someone who is having a panic attack, and never attempt to slap the person to "snap her out of it." Do not ask a patient to rebreathe her air from a paper bag as this can cause low blood oxygen levels.

1. **Remove the cause.** Try to find out the cause of the patient's fear and separate her from it. Either remove it from her or move her away from it.

2. **Be firm.** Try to calm the patient by talking firmly but kindly and calmly to her. Explain that she is having a panic attack and keep others away.

3. **Encourage her to breathe calmly.** Breathing more slowly will help to calm her and will stop her hyperventilating. Try to encourage her to copy your breathing pattern.

4. **Monitor patient.** Stay with her until she has recovered. If she has a history of panic attacks, advise her to seek help to learn how to control them.

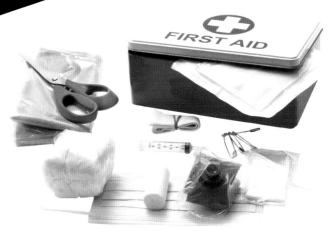

FIRST AID

Be prepared: Know what to do and how to do it.

BURNS AND SCALDS

Burns are caused by dry heat (fire or smoke), chemicals, or electricity and scalds by wet heat (hot water or steam). The skin is the body's natural infection barrier and is made up of several layers. Any break in the skin allows fluid to escape and germs to enter. This type of injury carries major risks: body fluids are lost from the circulatory system, and infection is likely because the body's protective layer is damaged. Your aim is to cool the burn as soon as possible to stop the burning process.

ESTABLISH THE SEVERITY OF THE BURN

- Severe pain at the site of injury, although deep burns may be pain-free

- Blisters around the site of the injury

- Redness and swelling at the site of injury, or charred skin if the burn is severe

TAKE CARE

- Put on disposable gloves if possible. Use latex-free gloves, as some people are allergic to latex.

- Do not cover the burn with plasters.

- Never put ointments or gels on a burn.

- Do not give the patient food or drink, as he may need an anesthetic later.

- If the patient becomes unconscious, open the airway and check breathing. Be prepared to begin CPR (see page 83).

- Seek medical advice for any burn larger than an inch. All deep burns or burns on children need hospital treatment.

- Monitor the patient's level of consciousness, breathing, and pulse while you wait for emergency help.

1. **Cool the burn.** Pour cool or tepid water over the burn for at least 10 minutes, or until the pain eases. Sit the patient down and raise the injured area. Make her as comfortable as possible. Call for emergency help.

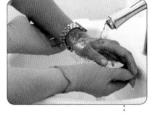

2. **Remove constrictions.** Remove or cut away any clothing or jewelry from the affected area while you are cooling it. Do not try to remove anything that is stuck to the burn.

3. **Protect the burn.** Cover the burn, ideally with plastic kitchen wrap or a clean plastic bag. If you do not have either of these available, use a sterile dressing large enough to cover the burn or a clean, non-fluffy material, such as a cotton pillowcase.

4. **Lay patient down.** Help the patient to lie down, while keeping the injured area raised and supported. Raise her legs above the level of her heart and support them on a chair. This reduces the risk of shock, a life-threatening condition that can develop after serious loss of fluids.

CHEMICALS

CHEMICAL ON SKIN

Contact with chemicals can result in very severe burns, which need urgent medical attention. Try to determine which chemical has caused the injury, as the information will help the medical team to decide on the most appropriate treatment. Protect yourself from contact with the chemical by wearing rubber gloves and protective clothing.

1. **Move patient to safety.** If the patient is inside, make sure that the area is well ventilated and any fumes are dispersed.

2. **Rinse affected area.** Pour water onto the burn for 20 minutes or longer—time this to ensure that you treat the injury for long enough. Pour the water away from yourself so that no chemical is washed onto your skin.

3. **Allow water to drain safely.** Make sure that the contaminated water can drain away safely; raise a patient's foot if necessary so that the water does not run over unaffected areas.

4. **Remove contaminated clothes.** Help the patient to remove any clothing that has become contaminated with the chemical while you are washing the area.

5. **Cover burn.** Cover the burn to protect it from infection and further fluid loss. Ideally cover it with plastic kitchen wrap or a plastic bag. Lay the film along the burn rather than wrapping it around a limb. If you do not have either of these, use a sterile wound dressing or lint-free cloth, such as a cotton pillowcase.

6. **Take to the hospital.** You can take the patient to the hospital or call emergency services depending on the extent

of the injury. Treat patient for shock if necessary (see page 107). Monitor the patient's condition. Check and make a note of her level of consciousness, breathing, and pulse.

7. **At the hospital, the burn will be assessed, and treatment will depend on the chemical involved.** The injury will be cleaned and dressed with a sterile gauze or dressing, and the patient will be offered pain relief. If the burn is severe, the patient will be referred to a specialist and may need to be admitted to the hospital.

CHEMICAL IN EYE

The severity of the burn depends on the substance involved and for how long it was in contact with the eye. Damage is usually limited to the front part of the eye, but there is a risk of internal injury. Try to identify the chemical.

1. **Protect yourself.** Put on protective gloves to protect yourself from contact with the chemical.

2. **Rinse eye.** Hold the patient's head under lukewarm running water for at least 10 minutes to wash out the chemical and prevent further damage. The affected eye should be lower than the good eye to prevent the chemical running into them both. If he cannot open his eye, gently hold the eyelids open.

3. **Cover eye.** Give the patient a sterile or clean pad to hold over the injured eye.

4. **Take to the hospital.** Take the patient to the hospital or call emergency services. Tell the medical team what substance caused the injury.

Safety at home

STORING CHEMICALS

Keep cleaning chemicals, dishwasher detergent, and washing powder out of reach of children—do not keep these items under the sink.

USE SAFETY CATCHES

Put safety catches on all cupboards containing chemicals. Choose chemicals with safety tops and leave them in their original bottles. Always keep garden chemicals in a locked shed.

USING CHEMICALS

Never combine chemicals (for example, toilet cleaner and bleach) when you are cleaning, as they can give off dangerous fumes. Do not put potentially toxic chemicals down in the parts of the garden where children and pets are playing or where they might play.

POTENTIALLY DANGEROUS HOUSEHOLD CHEMICALS

Caustic chemicals such as drain cleaner, some weed killers, bleach, and paint stripper need special care, as they can cause burns. Many other chemicals, such as kitchen cleaner, polish, washing powders, and conditioners, can cause an allergic reaction in some people. Always follow the instructions on the bottle, including the best course of action to follow in case of an accident.

ACCIDENTAL POISONING

The most common method of poisoning is by swallowing (ingestion). Many cases occur as a result of swallowing poisonous household products, which also cause burns. Most casualties are children, but the elderly are also at risk. Poisoning can also result from an accidental or, occasionally, deliberate overdose of over-the-counter, prescription, or recreational drugs.

Symptoms and signs will depend on what the person has swallowed, so it is important to establish the cause. Look for:

- Burns or blisters at the mouth if the poison is a corrosive substance

- Abdominal pains—these can be severe

- Empty containers, berries, or leaves near the patient

ADDITIONAL SYMPTOMS

- Vomiting and/or diarrhea—this may be bloodstained

- Signs of breathing difficulties

- Possible seizures

- Patient may not be fully conscious, and may lose consciousness at any time

Accidental poisoning can be life-threatening. If in any doubt, call 911 as soon as possible. If the victim has swallowed a chemical, protect yourself from contact with it by wearing rubber gloves and protective clothing. Use a protective mask if

POISONOUS SUBSTANCES

TYPE	WHAT TO WATCH FOR
COSMETICS AND CREAMS	Makeup, creams, and cleansers can be poisonous if swallowed.
MEDICINES	Overdoses of prescription drugs and over-the-counter medications, such as cough medicines, acetaminophen, aspirin, and ibuprofen.
HOUSEHOLD CHEMICALS	Bleach, carpet-cleaning products, and dishwasher detergent can cause burns; soap, furniture polish, and other household products are also poisonous.
PLANTS	Many plants are harmful, especially deadly nightshade, wild arum lily berries, yew, holly berries, laburnum, lupines, delphiniums, and foxgloves.
GARDEN CHEMICALS	Weed killer can cause burns; slug pellets and fertilizers are also poisonous.

an unconscious patient has burns on the lips and you have to give rescue breaths.

1. **Identify poison.** If the patient is conscious and able to talk, ask her what she took. If she is not fully conscious, look around for clues. Try to rouse the person and then encourage her to spit out anything that is in her mouth.

2. **Call emergency help.** Tell the dispatcher and the ambulance crew what the patient has swallowed, when she took it, and how much you think she took. Give them the container that the substance came in.

3. **Soothe burned lips.** If the patient has swallowed a corrosive poison, it may have burned her lips. Let her take small sips of cool milk or water to soothe the burns, but get her to spit it out.

4. **Wipe away vomit.** If the patient vomits, wipe her mouth clean, but do not give her anything to eat or drink. Help her to lean forward so that fluid can drain from her mouth

safely. Never attempt to induce vomiting, especially if the substance is corrosive. Anything that burned the gullet on the way down will burn it again on the way back up.

5. **Monitor patient.** Check and make a note of any change in her level of consciousness, breathing, and pulse while you are waiting for help to arrive. If the patient becomes unconscious, open the airway and check for breathing and be prepared to begin CPR.

SAFETY WITH POISONS

- **Poisonous plants.** A surprising number of garden plants have poisonous berries, leaves, or roots. If you have young children, consider fencing the plants off or even digging them up.

- **Medication.** Keep all medicines out of reach of children, preferably in a locked cabinet. Make sure that bottles have child-resistant caps. If a person is on regular medication but finds it difficult to remember which tablet to take and when to do so, consider putting pills in an automatic dispenser box to reduce the risk of an accidental overdose.

SPRAINED ANKLE

USE RICE TO REMEMBER TREATMENT STEPS

- **R**—Rest
- **I**—Ice
- **C**—Compression
- **E**—Elevation

A sprain occurs when one or more of the ligaments have been stretched, twisted, or torn—it is the most common ankle injury. In a minor sprain, some of the fibers within the ligament are stretched. In more serious sprains, the ligament may be torn. Minor sprains can be treated at home. Serious sprains need medical attention and may even require surgery.

A sprained ankle is a common injury, and the pain can be excruciating. If in doubt, take the injured person to the hospital for an X-ray.

WHAT TO LOOK FOR

- With a severe injury, the patient may not be able to bear weight on the leg

- Pain in and around the joint—the patient may feel faint with the pain

- Swelling, and later bruising, around the joint

1. **Rest leg.** The patient should stop the activity that caused the injury. Help her to sit down and rest the ankle. Support it in a raised position.

2. **Cool with ice.** Cool the injury to reduce pain and swelling. Make a cold compress (see page 154). Ideally wrap a bag of ice or frozen peas in a cloth and place it on the ankle. Do not put ice straight onto the skin, as

it will cause a cold burn. Leave the ice in place for about 20 minutes.

3. **Compression.** Leave the compress in place if it is small or wrap a layer of soft padding, such as a roll of cotton wool, around the ankle. Apply pressure with a compression support or compression bandage to help limit swelling. This should extend from the toes to the knee.

4. **Elevate ankle.** Raise and support the ankle so that it is higher than the hip to prevent swelling. Advise the patient to rest the ankle. If you suspect serious injury, take the patient to the hospital.

5. **Check circulation.** Make sure that the bandage is not too tight. Press on a toenail until it turns white, then let go: the color should return quickly. If it does not return, the bandage is too tight; remove it and reapply. Recheck every 10 minutes.

6. **Reapply the cold compress over the bandage every two to three hours.** Remove the bandage at night and do not sleep with an ice pack on the injury.

Folding triangular bandages

Folded lengthwise, these bandages can be used to provide support to an injured lower or upper limb. Narrow-fold bandages can also be used to help maintain pressure to control bleeding if you do not have a roller bandage. Open triangular bandages are used as slings, but do not exert enough pressure to control bleeding.

LAY BANDAGE FLAT.
Lay the bandage out on a flat surface with the longest edge facing you. Bring the top point down to touch the base.

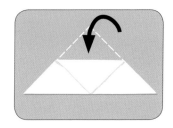

BROAD-FOLD BANDAGE:
Fold the bandage in half again to make a broad-fold bandage used to "splint" an injured limb to an uninjured part of the body.

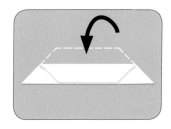

NARROW-FOLD BANDAGE:
Fold the bandage in half again. This narrow bandage is used to tie the feet and ankles together.

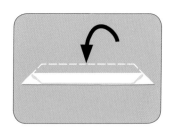

Tying a reef knot

A reef knot is used for tying bandages. It lies flat so that it is comfortable as well as secure. It is also very simple to undo quickly in an emergency.

1. **RIGHT OVER LEFT** Take the right-hand end over the left-hand end and pass it underneath.

2. **LEFT OVER RIGHT** Then pass what is now the left-hand end over the right-hand end and under.

3. **PULL TIGHT** Pull the ends gently to tighten the knot.

4. **TO UNDO THE KNOT** Hold the strands on one side of the knot (either both of the blue or both orange). Sharply pull both ends away from each other at the same time. Slide the straight section out of the knot.

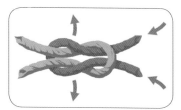

INJURED LOWER LIMB

An injury to the pelvis or lower limb—thigh, knee, and lower leg—is most commonly caused by a fall on a hard surface. Sprains and broken bones are common, while an injury to the pelvis or thighbone may lead to internal bleeding and shock.

It is always safer to treat the injury as a break. Signs and symptoms to look out for include:

- Deformity or swelling at site of injury

- One leg may be turned outward

- Severe pain at the site of the injury

- Patient may not be able to walk on injured leg.

- One leg may be shorter than the other; this is most likely following a fractured thigh, as the large muscles contract around the bone ends.

- Possible shock if a large bone, such as the thigh, is broken

Call emergency services as soon as possible. Avoid unnecessary movement. Do not give the patient anything to eat or drink, as an anesthetic may be required at the hospital.

LEG INJURY

1. **Support injured leg.** Do not let the patient walk. Hold the joints above and below the site of the injury. Ask a helper to put rolled blankets or towels either side of the injured leg.

2. **Call emergency help.** Ideally ask someone to make the call while you reassure the patient and support the injured leg.

3. **When help is delayed.** Provide extra support to the injured leg by immobilizing it. Place soft padding between

the legs and bring the uninjured leg to the injured one. Secure the feet and ankles using a narrow-fold bandage (see page 136) tied securely in a figure eight to prevent further movement. If you have help, ask the other person to do this for you while you support the joints.

4. **Add three more bandages.** Slide three broad-fold bandages (see page 136) under the natural hollows of the knees and ankles. Move the bandages into position: the first around the knees, the second above the fracture site, and the third below it. You must avoid the fracture site. The photograph shows a fractured lower leg. Tie reef knots (see page 137) against the uninjured leg or over the padding in the center.

- If there is a wound at the site of the break, or a bone is exposed, cover it with a piece of gauze, then build up padding either side of the bone until it is higher than the bone. Secure with a bandage.

- If the injury is near the ankle, then, instead of a figure eight bandage, use two narrow-fold bandages—one around the leg and one around the feet.

- If the injury is near the upper thigh, position the bandage above the injury so that it is around the hips, avoiding the fracture site.

- Stop bandaging if doing so causes the patient discomfort. Immobilize the limb with rolled coats, blankets, or cushions and wait for medical help.

- Always check the circulation in the limb beyond the bandages. If it is restricted, loosen the bandages and reapply or support as above.

KNEE INJURY

1. **Help patient to lie down.** Do not let the patient walk. Help her to lie down on her back with her knee in a comfortable position, probably slightly bent. She is likely to be in severe pain. Support the knee with pillows or rolled coats.

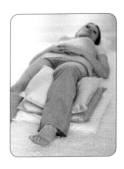

2. **For extra support.** Wrap some soft padding, such as cotton wool, around the knee and, if possible, secure it with a roller bandage that extends from mid calf to mid thigh. Stop immediately if this causes further pain.

3. **Call emergency help.** The patient needs to be transported on a stretcher in the treatment position (steps 1 and 2 above). Monitor the patient while you are waiting for help to arrive.

Occasionally it may be necessary to provide additional support to a patient who has a thigh injury—if for example you have to wait a long time for help. In this instance it can help to place a splint along the outside of the body.

- **Suitable materials.** Use something sturdy but not too bulky—a fence post, broom handle, or walking stick is ideal. The splint needs to extend from the patient's armpits to the feet. For additional comfort, place padding between the object and the limb before securing it.

- **Securing the splint.** Place the padding against the injured side and position the splint. Secure it using seven folded triangular bandages. Slide them under the natural hollows of the body and move them into position. Tie the first, a narrow-fold bandage, around the feet and ankles, then tie six broad-fold bandages as follows: the first around the knees, then around chest, pelvis, above and below the fracture site, and, finally, a bandage around the lower legs.

PELVIC INJURY

1. **Help patient to lie down.** Do not let the patient walk. Help him to lie down on his back if he is not lying down already. Carefully slide some folded towels, a cushion, or a rolled coat under his knees to raise them slightly. Stop if this causes the patient any discomfort.

2. **Immobilize legs.** Place soft padding between the knees and ankles. For extra comfort, slide a folded triangular bandage (see narrow-fold bandage, page 136) under his ankles. Tie the bandage in a figure eight around his feet and ankles to immobilize the legs and secure with a reef knot tied against the soles of his shoes.

3. **Immobilize legs.** Tie a second triangular bandage (see broad-fold bandage, page 136) around the knees for additional support. Do not move the patient unless his life is in immediate danger. Even then 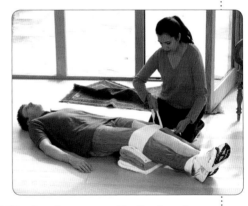 the legs must be immobilized and supported beforehand.

4. **Call emergency help.** The patient needs to be transported in the treatment position. Monitor him while you are waiting. Keep his head low to minimize the risk of shock, as there may be severe internal bleeding following a pelvic injury.

INJURED UPPER LIMB

Normally, considerable force is needed to break a bone, but force can also pull a joint out of place (dislocation), injure the bands of tissue, called ligaments, that hold a joint together (sprain), or tear or strain a muscle. If in doubt, treat this kind of injury as a break, as broken bone ends can damage surrounding tissues.

Unless you can see a bone end in a wound, it is impossible to know if a bone is broken without an X-ray. If any of the following symptoms are present, immobilize the injured limb and take or send the person to the hospital:

- Deformity or swelling at the site of injury; compare injured and uninjured arms

- Pain increased by movement

- Patient may be unable to bend the arm

- If the patient is supporting the arm and leaning toward the injured side, suspect injury to the collarbone or shoulder

- If one shoulder looks flatter when compared with the opposite one, the joint may be dislocated

- Possible wound near the broken bone

- Bone end may be protruding

If there is a wound, cover it with a dressing to protect it from infection and control bleeding by applying direct pressure (see page 173). If the bone is visible, press either side of the wound. Immobilize the joints above and below the wound, then raise and support the arm. Any patient with a suspected fracture or a dislocated joint must be taken to the hospital for treatment. Always immobilize the injury before transporting a person to minimize the risk of further injury.

Improvising slings

A sling can be improvised by using a scarf folded in half diagonally. Depending on the site of the injury you may also be able to use the patient's clothing.

JACKET "SLING"

If the patient is wearing a jacket, undo the fastenings. Ask the patient to support the injured arm and fold the lower half of the jacket up over the injured arm, making sure the elbow is supported. Secure the hem of the jacket to the top half with a safety pin. This is ideal for an injured forearm, wrist, or hand, as it provides the most support. If the patient has an upper arm injury, partially unbutton or unzip the jacket and slide the hand into the jacket opening. Secure the zip with a safety pin. Do not use this "sling" for a patient who has a forearm or wrist injury, as it does not provide sufficient support.

SLEEVE "SLING"

Help the patient to support the arm on the injured side in the most comfortable position, across the chest. Pin the sleeve cuff to the opposite side of the shirt or jacket. This can be useful for a shoulder or upper arm injury—do not use it if the patient has a wrist injury.

BELT "SLING"

Use a belt or long scarf folded into a thin strip. Fasten or tie into a loop, slip over the patient's head, and twist once to form a figure eight. Slip the lower loop over the patient's wrist. Do not use if the patient has a wrist injury.

SHOULDER/COLLARBONE

1. **Support arm with an elevation sling.** Help the patient to support the injured arm so that her fingers are touching the opposite shoulder. Place a triangular bandage over the arm with the longest edge parallel to her uninjured side and the top point at her shoulder. Tuck the longest edge under her injured arm.

2. **Secure sling at the shoulder.** Carry the lower point around the patient's back and up to the shoulder to meet the other point. Tie the ends in a reef knot just in front of the collarbone.

3. **Secure the corner.** Twist the corner of the bandage at the elbow until it fits the elbow snugly and tuck in the end to secure the sling. Check the circulation in the thumb after securing the sling. If it is restricted, loosen the sling and reapply, or simply support by hand.

4. **Take to the hospital.** If possible take the patient yourself, or call for emergency services if you have no transport. Do not give the patient anything to eat or drink, as he may need an anesthetic later.

CHILDREN AND THE ELDERLY

Children's bones are still growing so are softer than an adult's. As a result, the force that might break an adult's bone may cause a child's bone to partially break on one side and bend on the other, like a twig. This is known as a greenstick fracture. The injury needs to be treated in the same way as any other break.

Conversely, the bones of an elderly person are more fragile and it can take comparatively little force to break a bone.

ARM INJURY

1. **Support arm.** Gently place the patient's arm across her body. Encourage her to support it herself; help her if necessary. Help her to sit down.

2. **Immobilize with an arm sling.** Carefully slide a triangular bandage between the patient's arm and her chest so that the longest side is along the uninjured side. Take the top corner around the back of the patient's neck to the front of the shoulder on the injured side.

3. **Protect injury.** Wrap soft padding—a small towel for example, around the site of the injury for extra support. Bring the lower part of the triangular bandage up over the arm and tie a reef knot just over the hollow in front of the shoulder.

4. **Secure.** Twist the excess fabric at the elbow so that the sling fits around it, then tuck the end into the fabric. The weight of the arm in the sling will hold it in place.

5. **Take to the hospital.** If possible take the patient yourself, or call for emergency services if you have no transport.

INJURY NEAR ELBOW

1. **Support arm.** If the injury is near the elbow, the patient will not be able to bend his arm. Help him to sit down and support his arm in the position that feels most comfortable. Tell him to avoid unnecessary movement. If one or more bones are broken, the jagged ends could damage the blood vessels or nerves around the joint. If there is a wound, cover it with a dressing to minimize the risk of infection and bandage it in place. If there is a bone sticking out of the wound, loosely drape a piece of gauze over the top. Place padding on either side and bandage over the top.

2. **Protect arm.** Wrap soft padding around the outside of the joint—a small towel is ideal.

3. **Immobilize the injury.** For additional comfort, tie two broad-fold bandages (see page 136) or large scarves around the arm and body. Place one bandage above the elbow and the other around the forearm.

4. **Check the circulation.** Check the pulse at the wrist and loosen the bandages if there is no pulse.

5. **Take to the hospital.** If possible take the patient yourself or call for emergency services if you have no transport.

WRIST AND HAND INJURY

A typical wrist and hand injury results from a fall onto an outstretched hand, when a bone in the forearm is broken at the wrist. Known as a colles fracture, it is most common in the elderly. Wrists may also be sprained, and the small bones in the wrist, hand, or fingers may be injured through crushing, in which case bleeding can be profuse.

It is difficult to tell whether the wrist is sprained or a bone is broken without an X-ray. If in doubt, always take the patient to the hospital. Look for:

- Severe pain at the site of injury, increased by movement

- Swelling, and later bruising, around the injured area

- Open wound and bleeding following a crush injury

Cover a wound with a sterile dressing to protect it from infection, and control bleeding by applying direct pressure. If the bone is visible, press on either side of the wound. If a patient's hand has been crushed and is still trapped, free it only if you know the incident happened recently.

1. **Support arm.** Gently place the patient's arm across her body. Encourage her to support it herself. Help her to sit down. If the patient has injured her hand, treat any wounds (see page 172).

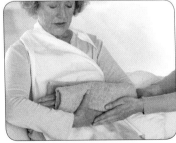

2. **Immobilize forearm in an arm sling.** Slide a triangular bandage between the patient's arm and her chest so that the longest side is parallel with the

uninjured side. Take the top corner around the patient's neck to the front of the shoulder on the other side. After immobilizing the arm, check for a pulse at the wrist. If there is no pulse, remove the sling and support the injury by hand and/or cushions.

3. **Protect injury.** Place soft padding around the site of injury for extra support. Bring the lower part of the bandage up over the arm and secure the sling in front of the shoulder.

4. **Take to the hospital.** If the patient is uncomfortable, provide extra support by securing the arm to the body with a broad-fold bandage (see page 136). You can take the patient to the hospital or call for emergency services if you have no transport.

BACK AND NECK INJURY

The column of bones (vertebrae) in the back and neck supports the body and protects the delicate spinal cord. A back or neck injury can fracture one or more of the vertebrae or injure the muscles. Serious injury can damage the spinal cord, which could result in permanent loss of movement to any part of the body below that point. If a person falls awkwardly onto her head, back, or neck, suspect spine injury until you are told otherwise. It is safer to immobilize her than risk permanent injury by moving her. Look for:

- Fall from a height—for example, off a ladder or from a horse

- Severe pain in the neck or back

- Signs of head injury

- Feeling of heaviness in the limbs, or inability to move or feel them

- Inability to move or feel any part of the body

- Signs of loss of bladder control

- Possible irregularity along spine

Do not move the patient unless her life is in immediate danger. If the person is unconscious, do not tilt the head to open the airway, use the jaw thrust (see next page). Then check her breathing. Do not give the patient anything to eat or drink, as she may need an anesthetic when she reaches the hospital. If she is thirsty, moisten her lips with water.

1. **Call emergency help.** Reassure the patient and ideally ask someone else to call for emergency services while you support the head.

2. **Immobilize patient.**
   Kneel or lie behind her
   head, place your elbows
   on your knees or on the
   ground. Leaving her head
   in the position you found
   her, place your hands on

   either side of her head to support it. Be careful not to cover
   her ears, as she needs to hear you talking to her.

3. **Get extra support.** Ask
   someone to get some rolled
   blankets, towels, or coats
   and place them on either
   side of the patient's head
   for additional support until
   emergency services arrive.

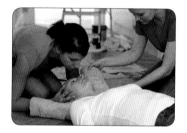

4. **Monitor patient.** Stay at her head and ask your helper
   to check and make a note of her level of consciousness,
   breathing, and pulse. Recheck regularly until medical
   help arrives.

Opening the airway of a neck injury patient

If a patient with suspected back or neck injury is not breathing, do not tilt
the head to open the airway, as it is important to keep her back and neck
in a straight line. Instead, use a technique called the jaw thrust.

- **Support patient's head.** Resting your
  elbows on your knees or on the ground,
  place your hands on either side of her head
  and keep it in line with her body.

- **Push the jaw upward.** Place your
  fingertips on either side at the angle of the
  lower jaw and "push" it upward (toward the
  ceiling) and forward.

- **Check breathing.** Look, listen, and feel for signs of breathing for no more
  than 10 seconds. Be prepared to begin CPR (see pages 83–86).

BLOW TO THE HEAD

Any blow to the head is potentially serious. A comparatively minor bump could affect a person's level of consciousness. Brain tissue or blood vessels inside the skull could also be damaged but the effects may not be apparent. A person may appear to be fine, then develop a headache or collapse later on. Anyone with a head injury may also have a spine injury. It is always better to be safe—seek medical advice even if the patient appears to be unharmed by the blow to the head. Assess her carefully. In particular, watch for any change in her condition. Signs of potentially serious injury to look out for include:

- Mild headache initially that becomes progressively worse, or sudden severe headache

- No recollection of recent events and/or the incident

- Confusion and uncharacteristic behavior; she may become very irritable

- A brief period of unconsciousness

- Serious wound to any part of the face or head

- Depressed area of the skull following an injury indicates a possible skull fracture. There may also be watery blood leaking from the nose or ear.

- Breathing becomes noisy and/or slow

- Slow, but strong pulse

- Pupils become unequal in size

- Patient becomes drowsy; she may become unconscious

Stay with a patient who has sustained a head injury. Do not let a patient go home on her own after a head injury. Do not give any alcohol. Seek medical advice if the patient needs to take prescription medication. A person who is injured on the sports field should rest and must not be allowed to play on even if he claims to have recovered. If the patient needs medical treatment, do not give him anything to eat or drink, as he may need an anesthetic. If he is thirsty, moisten his lips with water.

THE RISKS OF HEAD INJURY

- **Concussion.** A blow to the head can cause the brain to be shaken within the skull—known as concussion. This shaking causes a temporary disturbance in the brain, which can result in the patient becoming unconscious for a short time. The patient normally recovers completely but may not remember what happened. However, a more serious brain injury—compression—could develop later.

- **Compression.** Compression injury results when there is a buildup of pressure against the brain within the skull. This can follow a severe blow to the head that results in skull fracture. But, for example, it can be caused by bleeding between the brain and the skull after an apparently minor blow, swelling within the brain, a stroke, or a brain tumor. Symptoms may be apparent immediately or may develop hours or even days later. It is life-threatening; the patient will deteriorate and almost always needs surgery.

1. **Sit patient down.** Assess the patient's level of consciousness. If he is fully conscious, help him to sit down, ideally on the floor, so that he cannot fall. Make him comfortable.

2. **Place cold pack on injury.** Give him a pack of ice (wrapped in a cloth) to place against the injury. If the person was knocked out, even if only for a very short time, seek medical advice.

3. **If there is a scalp wound apply direct pressure.** Place a sterile pad over the wound and apply pressure directly over it. Help the patient onto the floor into a half-sitting position so that her head is positioned above her heart. Secure the pad with a bandage wrapped around the head to maintain pressure on the wound (see also Wounds and Bleeding, page 172). Take the patient to hospital or call for emergency help.

4. **Monitor patient.** Tell the patient to rest quietly. Stay with him. If he does not recover completely within half an hour, or begins to deteriorate at any point, call for emergency services at once. If a patient remains conscious, make sure that someone stays with him for at least 24 hours after the injury. If the patient is not fully conscious, help him to lie down and place him in the recovery position. Call emergency services.

Severe head injuries always require treatment in hospital. The patient will be assessed by the medical team and diagnosis will be confirmed with brain scans. Further treatment will depend on the severity of the injury.

Children are particularly prone to head injuries, as they have high energy levels and little sense of danger. To protect a child from head injuries when cycling, he should always wear a cycling helmet.

SEVERE BRUISING

A bruise is a closed wound in which bleeding from damaged blood vessels is trapped in the tissues, causing bluish-black discoloration. Depending on the force of the blow, there may be additional injuries. Bruising may not appear immediately.

A person taking a blood-thinning medication (anticoagulant), such as warfarin, for a medical condition is at risk of severe bruising because the medication can prevent clotting. Internal bleeding may be identified only by signs of shock (see page 107) that develop with no visible bleeding. Call emergency services if you suspect serious internal injury.

Bruising is most commonly the result of bleeding from the smallest blood vessels (the capillaries) and in some instances appears a few days after an injury. If a large blood vessel is damaged, swelling will be more severe. Signs of severe bruising include:

- Bluish discoloration

- Swelling and discomfort

- Severe pain at site of injury

If unexplained bruises occur easily or for no apparent reason, especially if accompanied by frequent nosebleeds or bleeding gums, seek medical advice.

MAKING A COLD COMPRESS

Cooling an injury with ice slows down the metabolism within the tissue, reducing bleeding, muscle spasm, and inflammation (and therefore pain), so aiding recovery. Place a cold compress on an injury for 10–20 minutes at a time—don't leave it for any longer. Repeat this procedure every 2–3 hours; it is most effective in the first 48 hours after injury. Never put ice directly onto the skin because it can cause a cold burn.

- **Making an ice pack.** Fill a plastic bag with ice cubes or crushed ice. Seal the bag, then wrap it in a hand towel or dishcloth. Alternatively, you can use a bag of frozen peas or corn, as it will mold well to the shape of the body.

- **Making a cold pack.** If you do not have any ice, soak a small towel in cold water and wring it out, then place it over the injury. Keep it cool by dripping cold water over it at regular intervals.

1. **Rest the injury.** Tell the patient to stop his current activity and rest. Raise the injury, as this reduces blood flow to the area.

2. **Cool the injury.** Place a cold compress over the injury. Leave it in place for up to 20 minutes.

3. **Comfortable support.** Tell the patient to keep the injury raised to rest the affected part. Wrap padding around the injury and apply a compression bandage if the pain is severe (see page 135).

4. **Elevate the injury.** Rest and support the injury in a raised position to minimize swelling. Apply a sling to an arm injury if necessary (see page 143).

If several small bruises subsequently form around a large one, and the patient has not had any other accidents, he should seek medical advice immediately to find out whether his blood is clotting as it should. Also seek medical advice if the bruise is accompanied by swelling and severe pain and the person is taking a blood-thinning medication (anticoagulant).

CHEST INJURY

A framework of bones called the rib cage surrounds and protects the organs of the chest as well as major blood vessels. The chest may be injured by an external force from a fall or traffic incident or even during an assault. It is important to immobilize the injured side: if a rib is broken, the bone end could pierce a lung, blood vessel, or the chest wall.

Anyone with a suspected rib injury should be assessed at a hospital. Sometimes the ribs are not broken, but there is bruising of ribs or nearby muscles. Rib fractures may (but don't always) show on a chest X-ray. If a rib fracture is suspected, the main purpose of the X-ray is to look for complications rather than to diagnose the fracture itself.

SYMPTOMS AND SIGNS OF CHEST INJURY

- Possible chest wound near site of injury

- Pain in one or both sides of the chest worsened by movement, breathing, or coughing

- Swelling and deformity at site of injury may indicate a fractured rib

- Wound on the chest caused by fractured rib or injury that pierces chest wall, such as stabbing

- Evidence of bruising on injured side

A chest injury is potentially serious, as it can cause breathing difficulties. If a wound penetrates the chest wall, air can enter and a lung could collapse. The following should be treated as emergencies:

- **Difficulty breathing.** The person may be coughing, gasping for breath, and finding it difficult to talk. Skin may become gray-blue (known as cyanosis). This is especially noticeable at the ears, lips, inside the mouth, and at the fingertips.

- **Flail chest.** Normal chest movement may be reversed over the damaged area on the injured side. This is known as flail chest.

- **Rapid breathing.** Breathing may become fast and shallow; the patient appears frightened, while struggling to breathe.

- **Wound to chest wall.** This can be caused by a broken rib or an injury that pierces the chest wall.

- **Coughing up blood.** If a lung is injured, the patient may cough up bright red frothy blood and tell you there is a crackling sound. You may see blood bubbling from a wound and hear air being sucked in and out of it.

- **Goes into shock.** Symptoms and signs of shock may be evident.

IF THERE IS A WOUND
Protect yourself and the patient by wearing nonlatex disposable gloves.

1. **Place in half-sitting position.** Help the patient to sit on the floor. Place a sterile pad against the wound and ask the patient to hold it against him. Lean him toward the injured side and support him with cushions.

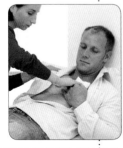

2. **Cover wound.** Place a sterile dressing over the wound. Cover the dressing with a sheet of plastic kitchen wrap or aluminum foil, secured with tape on three sides only. This allows air to escape from

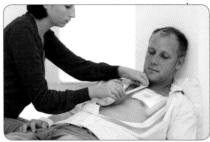

the chest but also prevents more from being sucked into the wound. The covering should be taut.

3. **Call for emergency help.** Call emergency services. Check and make a note of the patient's level of consciousness, breathing, and pulse. Recheck regularly until medical help arrives. If the person needs to be put in the recovery position, place him on his injured side, as this helps to stabilize the chest wall.

NO EXTERNAL WOUND

1. **Support arm on injured side.** Tell the patient to support the arm on the injured side; help him if necessary. Encourage him to sit down. Support the arm in a sling (see page 143) to stabilize the chest wall and minimize the risk of further damage.

2. **Take to hospital.** You can take the patient to hospital yourself or call for emergency services if you have no transport.

If a patient develops breathing difficulties after sustaining a chest injury, call emergency services immediately. Do not give the patient anything to eat or drink, as he may need treatment requiring an anesthetic later at the hospital.

If a patient becomes unconscious, open the airway and check breathing. If he needs to be placed in the recovery position, roll him onto his injured side, as this helps to stabilize the injured chest wall and enables the uninjured lung to work normally.

AMPUTATION

Fingers and toes—and even larger body parts such as arms—that are partially or completely severed in an accident can sometimes be reattached. It is vital to preserve the amputated part. The medical team will assess the extent of the damage.

1. **Control bleeding.** Wear nonlatex disposable gloves if you have them to protect yourself and the patient. Place a sterile wound dressing or clean pad on the wound, apply direct pressure and raise the affected area. Secure the pad with a bandage.

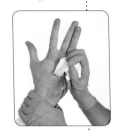

2. **Treat for shock.** Keeping the injured area elevated, help the patient to lie down on the ground. Raise and support his legs.

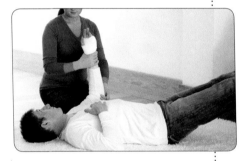

3. **Call emergency help.** Tell the dispatcher that it is an amputation.

4. **Monitor patient.** Check and make a note of his level of consciousness, breathing, and pulse. Recheck regularly until help arrives. Watchpoint: Do not give the patient anything to eat or drink, as he will need an anesthetic later in the hospital. If he is thirsty moisten his lips with water.

5. **Preserve the severed part.** Do not wash or rinse the part. Put the part in a plastic bag or wrap it in plastic kitchen wrap to keep it clean and prevent it from drying out. Wrap a soft cloth or towel around it.

6. **Put it in ice.** Place the wrapped part in a container full of ice (crushed is ideal). Make sure that the ice does not touch the surface of the part. Mark the package with the patient's name and time of the incident. Give the package to the emergency services.

ELECTRICAL INJURY

Contact with domestic low-voltage electricity or lighting is often the cause of an electrical injury, usually a burn. The electrical current needs breaking before help can be given. If the patient has been thrown by the current, there may be a fracture; if unconscious, the heart may stop. An incident with high-voltage electricity, such as power cables, is often fatal.

Assess the extent of the patient's injuries—in particular, check to see if there is more than one burn. Symptoms to note are:

- Superficial, partial or full-thickness burns (see page 126). There may be a second burn (an exit burn) where the electric current left the body

- Internal injury along the path of the electricity

- Symptoms and signs of shock if burns are severe (see page 107)

- Signs of upper and lower limb injury (see pages 138–146) or possibly back and neck injury (see page 149) if the patient was thrown by the electrical current

- Patient may be unconscious

HOW TO BREAK THE CONTACT WITH ELECTRICITY

If a patient is still in contact with the cause of the injury, you too will sustain an electric shock if

WARNING

- Do not touch a patient who remains in contact with the source of electricity.

- Do not touch a patient with wet hands.

- Do not go within 20 yards of a person who has been struck by high-voltage electricity unless the authorities have officially told you that the supply has been switched off.

- Do not approach a patient who is found near a high-voltage power line or overhead cable. Call emergency services and keep any bystanders away.

- Wear nonlatex disposable gloves if you have them to protect yourself and the patient.

you touch her. Low-voltage alternating current (AC) can cause muscle spasm, so the person will still be grasping the appliance that caused the electric shock.

- **Turn off the main supply.** First, try to turn off the electric current. This can normally be done by switching the supply off at the main. If successful you can approach the patient.

- **Move the source away from the patient.** If you cannot find the main switch, remove the source from the patient using a length of wood, which is nonconductive. Stand on a thick book, such as a  telephone directory, a stack of newspapers, or some similar dry insulating material. Use the wood to push the object away from contact with the patient.

- **Pull the patient away.** If neither of the first options is successful, stand on the insulating material. Loop a rope around the patient's legs and attempt to pull her clear.

1. **Break electrical contact.** Assess the area carefully before you approach to make sure the patient is no longer holding the electrical appliance.

2. **Cool burns.** Stop the burning process. Hold the injury under cool running water for at least 10 minutes, or until the pain eases. Remove the patient's watch, jewelry, or any tight clothing that might restrict swelling. Do not remove anything that is stuck to the wounds.

3. **Cover burns.** Cover the burns to protect them from infection and further fluid loss. Use plastic kitchen film, laid along the burn—do not wrap it around a limb. Cover a hand or foot with a plastic bag. Tape it closed, making sure the tape is on the plastic not the skin. If you do not have either of these, use a sterile wound dressing or clean, non-fluffy cloth, such as a cotton pillowcase.

4. **Treat any other injuries.** Attend to any other injuries, such as fractures, that the patient has sustained in the incident. Watch the patient for signs of shock and treat as necessary.

5. **Call emergency help.** Monitor the patient while you are waiting. Check and make a note of the level of consciousness, breathing, and pulse. Recheck regularly until help arrives. If the patient becomes unconscious, open the airway and check for breathing. Be prepared to begin CPR (see page 83).

PREVENTION

- Check electrical appliances regularly; this is especially important in an elderly person's home. Old appliances can be a fire risk.

- If you have young children in the home, put safety covers into unused electrical outlets.

- Do not overload outlets or extension cords.

- Use extension cords with "gangs" of outlets rather than single outlet adapters to reduce the risk of overloading a outlet.

- Always use adapters and extension cords that have circuit breakers.

- Fix wires to the baseboard; never let them trail across the floor.

- Check wiring regularly; throw away appliances with cracked or damaged cords.

- Make sure that appliances have sealed plugs.

- Keep electrical appliances away from water. Never touch appliances with wet hands.

- If a plug becomes warm when an appliance is switched on, it is faulty and should be replaced.

EYE INJURY

Eye injuries are usually the result of a scratch or graze caused by grit or a contact lens. Most injuries affect the transparent outer layer of the eye (cornea), which covers and protects the colored part of the eye (iris) and lets light into the hole in the center (pupil). These injuries need medical attention, as they can result in temporary or permanent loss of sight.

Eye injuries are potentially serious, as the patient's sight can be damaged. Examine the eye very carefully. Small, loose pieces of dust can often be picked off by the patient or rinsed off. The following are signs of serious injury:

- Severe pain in and around the eye

- An accident where the eye has been scratched by a thorn or small foreign body, such as a stone thrown up by a lawnmower

- Foreign object on the colored part of the eye

- Obvious wound, especially if there is fluid leaking from the eye

Do not try to remove anything that is sticking to the colored part of the eye. Call emergency services if the patient experiences a sudden loss of vision as a result of the injury.

1. **Support patient's head.** Tell the patient to keep her head as still as possible. Help her to lie down. Kneel behind her head and support her head on your lap to prevent unnecessary movement.

2. **Cover the eye.** Give the patient a sterile wound dressing or clean pad to hold over the affected eye. Tell her not to move her eyes; if she moves the good eye the injured one will also move.

3. **Reassure the patient.** Keep the patient as calm as you can. Do not give her anything to eat or drink, as treatment requiring an anesthetic may be needed when she reaches the hospital.

4. **Take to the hospital.** Try to keep the patient in the treatment position (see steps 1 and 2) on the way. Call emergency services if you have no transport.

5. **Bandage the eye.** If you have to wait a while for transport, the patient may be more comfortable if you secure the dressing with a bandage.

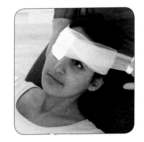

A superficial eye injury that does not penetrate the eye membrane will usually take 24–72 hours to heal, depending on the size of the abrasion. The injury may be treated with eye drops to prevent infection. The patient will be referred to an eye specialist if her vision is affected, if the eye socket or eyeball is injured, or if there is damage to the retina at the back of the eye.

BLACK EYE

A black eye develops when blood and other fluids collect in the space around the eye; resulting in swelling and the typical dark discoloration.

Most black eyes heal on their own and the eye itself is not injured. Sometimes the bruising signifies a more serious eye injury and there is a risk of long-term damage.

SIGNS THAT CAUSE CONCERN

- Fluid leaking from the eye

- Patient complains of blurred vision in the affected eye

- The affected eye appears to be a different shape from the other one

1. **Sit patient down.** Tell the patient to stop her current activity and rest.

2. **Cool the injury.** Give the patient a cold compress (see page 154) to hold against the affected area for 10–20 minutes.

3. **Monitor patient.** Check and make a note of her level of consciousness, breathing, and pulse. Make a note of any change in her condition.

4. **Take to the hospital.** If the patient's condition deteriorates, or there is serious injury to the eye, take her to the hospital or call emergency services.

SEVERE NOSEBLEED

Nosebleeds are fairly common, especially in children. They usually happen as a result of a minor injury, nose picking, or blowing the nose. Very occasionally, nosebleeds can be a sign of underlying illness or injury.

Very rarely a nosebleed can be life-threatening, especially in older people.

WHEN TO SEEK MEDICAL ADVICE

- Frequent nosebleeds (more than one a week); this can be a symptom of high blood pressure

- Persistent nosebleeds in a person who is on blood-thinning medication such as warfarin

- Thin watery blood from the nose following a blow to the head, which can indicate a possible skull fracture

- Frequent nosebleeds accompanied by bleeding gums as well as bruises that develop for no apparent reason

1. **Sit patient down.** Help the patient to sit down. Tell her to lean forward (she should not lean back) so that the blood can drain. Wear nonlatex disposable gloves if you have them to protect yourself and the patient.

2. **Pinch the nose.** Tell the patient to breathe through her mouth and pinch the soft part of her nose to help reduce blood flow. She can lean over a sink or give her a bowl so that she can spit out any blood; swallowing it can make her sick. Advise her not to sniff, swallow, or cough, as it can disturb the clots that are forming.

3. **Check nose.** After 10 minutes release the pressure and check the nose. If it is still bleeding, pinch the nose again for another 10 minutes.

4. **Offer a cold compress.** Give the patient an ice or cold pack (see page 154) to hold against the bridge of her nose to help reduce the blood flow.

5. **Check nose again.** Once bleeding has stopped, let the patient clean around her nose with a damp cloth. Tell her not to blow her nose and to avoid strenuous activity for up to 12 hours.

HELPING A YOUNG CHILD
A very young child may not be able to pinch her nose for long enough. Help her to sit forward and pinch her nose for her. Reassure her, get her to spit into a bowl, and wipe her face.

ITEMS IN EAR OR NOSE

Children often put small objects into the nose or ear. Sharp items can easily damage the lining of the nose or structures of the ear, while the acid in small batteries could even cause burns. If an object is not removed, it could lead to internal injury and possible infection. A sharp object in the ear may pierce the eardrum, leading to possible deafness.

Look into the nose or ear with a flashlight. If you see anything, take the patient to hospital.

IF THE OBJECT IS IN THE EAR

- Temporary deafness

- Patient will feel movement if it is an insect and may be very frightened. You may be able to see the insect float out.

1. **Take to the hospital.** If the person has an object in his ear or an insect is stuck, take him to the hospital. Call emergency services if you have no transport.

2. **Reassure the patient.** Keep the patient as calm as you can on your way to the hospital. Do not give him anything to eat or drink, as treatment requiring an anesthetic may be needed.

IF THE OBJECT IS IN THE NOSE

You may notice these symptoms:

- Pain if a sharp object is lodged in the nose

- Difficulty breathing through one nostril

- Swelling on one side of the nose

- Possible smelly discharge if the object has been there for some time

1. **Reassure the patient.** Tell the patient to breathe through the other nostril or his mouth. Keep him as calm as possible. Do not let him poke inside his nose to try to release the object.

2. **Take to the hospital.** You can take the patient to the nearest hospital yourself or call emergency services if you have no transport. Do not give the patient anything to eat or drink, as an anesthetic may be needed when he reaches the hospital.

INSECT STUCK IN THE EAR

If an insect flies or crawls into a person's ear, it may be possible to float it out. Put a towel around the patient's shoulders, tilt his head so that the affected ear is uppermost, and gently pour tepid water into the ear. As the ear is flooded the insect should come to the surface. If this does not work, you should take the patient to the hospital.

WOUNDS AND BLEEDING

A wound is a break in the skin that allows blood to escape from the body. Bleeding is potentially serious as fluid is lost from the circulatory system. Bleeding from the smallest blood vessels—the capillaries—is usually minor. However, if the larger vessels, the arteries and veins, are damaged, significant life-threatening blood loss can result very quickly.

The principles of first aid are the same whatever the site of blood loss. Blood loss is faster when a larger vessel is damaged.

- Blood loss from an artery is often bright red and, if a major vessel is damaged, blood may be spurting from the wound in time with the heartbeat

- Blood loss from a vein will be darker red and, if a larger vein is damaged, may gush profusely

- In some parts of the body, nerves and tendons can run very close to blood vessels and may be damaged. As a result the patient may experience loss of movement or feeling

TAKE CARE

- Always wear nonlatex disposable gloves if you have them to protect yourself and the patient from infection.

- Always seek medical advice if a person who is taking a blood-thinning medication (anticoagulants) for a medical condition has a minor injury, as he will bleed more profusely.

- Apply pressure directly over an injury or on either side if there is an object stuck in the wound. Never use indirect pressure, as it will cut off the blood supply.

- If signs of shock appear (see page 107), call emergency services immediately. Make a note of the patient's level of consciousness, breathing, and pulse. Recheck regularly until medical help arrives.

- If blood seeps through a dressing, cover it with another one, secured with a second bandage. If blood comes through the second bandage, you may not be applying pressure at the right point. Take off both dressings and apply a new one.

- If the patient becomes unconscious, open the airway and check for breathing. Be prepared to begin CPR (see page 83).

- Do not give the patient anything to eat or drink, as he may need an anesthetic later.

SEVERE BLEEDING

1. **Apply direct pressure.** Place a sterile wound dressing or clean pad against the wound and press firmly. Remove or cut away clothing to expose the wound if necessary.

2. **Raise and support injury.** Raise the injured part so that it is higher than the patient's heart. This will slow down the blood flow to the area.

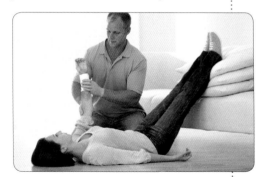

3. **Treat for shock.**
Help the patient to lie down, while keeping the injured area raised and supported. Raise and support her legs above the level of her heart, on a bed or chair, for example. This reduces the risk of shock (see page 107). Keep the legs straight and rest her ankles or heels on the bed or chair to prevent blood pooling in her legs.

4. **Bandage.** Tie a bandage around the dressing. Support an arm in a sling (see page 143) for extra support. Call emergency services.

WOUND ON THE PALM

1. **Cover wound with dressing pad.** Place a large sterile dressing pad into the palm of the patient's hand, preferably the type with a bandage attached. Ask her to clench her fist tightly over the pad to apply pressure. Raise and support her hand.

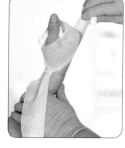

2. **Secure dressing.** Wind the bandage around the patient's clenched fist, leaving the thumb exposed. Secure the bandage over the top of the fingers to maintain pressure. Check the circulation in the thumb (see page 135).

AT INNER ELBOW OR KNEE

1. **Bend arm or leg.** Place a sterile dressing pad over the injury and bend the arm or leg over it to apply pressure. Raise the injured part to slow down the blood flow further.

2. **Check circulation.** As raising the affected limb and applying pressure to the wound can severely reduce the blood supply to the rest of the limb, check the circulation

in the lower arm or leg every 10 minutes, releasing the pressure if necessary.

BLEEDING FROM VARICOSE VEINS

Veins in the legs have one-way valves that prevent back flow of blood as it returns from the tissues to the heart. If these valves fail, blood pools in the veins, resulting in varicose veins. The veins are often near the surface and can burst following a relatively minor knock, causing life-threatening profuse bleeding.

1. **Raise injured leg.** Help the patient to lie down on the floor and raise his leg as high as you can—this will immediately slow down the bleeding. Ideally, rest the leg on your shoulder.

2. **If a patient is wearing elastic-topped stockings, remove them.** Releasing the grip stops the bleeding.

3. **Apply direct pressure.** Keeping the leg raised, place a sterile dressing pad over the wound and press firmly until the bleeding is under control.

4. **Secure dressing.** If necessary, place another dressing and bandage over the first one. Bandage dressings firmly in place. To ensure the bandage is not too tight, check circulation in the foot (see page 135). If necessary, loosen the bandages and reapply.

5. **Call for emergency help.** Call emergency services, as the patient needs to go to the hospital in the treatment position. Keep the leg raised until the medical team arrives.

IMPALEMENT

If a person becomes impaled on an object, moving the patient (or the object) can worsen the injury and cause increased pain. Find out how and when the person became impaled and which body part is affected.

Look out for signs of external or internal bleeding and symptoms and signs of shock. Make sure that you are not putting yourself in any danger by approaching the patient. Protect yourself and the patient by wearing nonlatex disposable gloves if you have them.

1. **Call for help.** Provide as much information as possible.

2. **Support patient.** Make the person as comfortable as you can; support the body by hand or with cushions, if possible, to ease discomfort. Do not move the patient or attempt to remove the object.

3. **Reassure patient.** Tell him that help is on the way. Check and make a note of the level of consciousness, breathing, and pulse. Recheck regularly until medical help arrives.

4. **Do not give the patient anything to eat or drink, as an anesthetic may be needed later in the hospital.**

5. **If the patient becomes unconscious, open the airway and check breathing.** If he is breathing and placing him in the recovery position is difficult, maintain a chin lift position to keep his airway open.

MOUTH WOUND

Wounds in the mouth are mostly minor and look worse than they are because they bleed profusely. They are often the result of a patient biting her own tongue and/or lip during a fall. In some cases, a tooth may be knocked out. Prompt first aid can prevent a patient inhaling blood, which could cause breathing difficulties.

Most mouth wounds can be treated at home, although those that are more severe may need the attention of a doctor or dentist. These are indicated by:

- Severe bleeding from lips or inside the mouth

- History of recent tooth extraction or any other facial injury

- Loss of tooth

If bleeding has not stopped after half an hour, or it restarts, take the patient to the hospital. If a patient has suffered a blow to the head, watch for signs of serious injury (see page 151).

1. **Sit patient down.** Help her to lean forward so that she does not inhale blood accidentally.

2. **Wear nonlatex disposable gloves if you have them to protect yourself and the patient.** Place pad against injury. Give the patient a pad to hold against the injury. If the wound is on the lips or inside the cheek, tell her to pinch the pad over the injury between her finger and thumb.

3. **For bleeding tooth socket.** Roll up a small piece of gauze and place it in the gap. Tell the patient to bite on the pad to apply pressure.

4. **Check the mouth.** After 10 minutes, check the mouth. If the injury is still bleeding, tell her to reapply pressure for

another 10 minutes. Advise her to spit out any blood that has accumulated in her mouth.

5. **Check tooth.** If a tooth has been knocked out, preserve it (see box). Take the patient to a dentist or hospital for possible reimplantation.

Care of knocked-out tooth

An adult, or second, tooth can often be reimplanted if it is not damaged. Do not wash the tooth however dirty it appears to be. Take the patient to a dentist or hospital where they can assess the possibility of replanting the tooth as well as damage to the bone or gum.

- **Keeping the tooth safe:** Once bleeding has stopped and as long as the person is fully conscious, tell her to put the tooth in the empty socket. If she cannot do this, tell her to put it in the side of her mouth against her cheek, taking care not to swallow it.

- **Preserve in milk.** If it is not safe to put the tooth in the patient's mouth, put it in a container of milk—not water.

- **Children's teeth.** A child's milk (first) tooth cannot be replaced, but second teeth can be reimplanted. Preserve the tooth as described above and take the child to the dentist with the preserved tooth.

INHALING FUMES

The inhalation of fumes can be life-threatening, as they reduce the amount of oxygen available to the body. A patient needs urgent medical help, but rescue should only be carried out by someone wearing protective breathing apparatus. Never enter a fume-filled room or building even if there are casualties. Call for emergency help. Ask for the fire department and tell the controller there are fumes.

Any patient will have very low levels of oxygen in her body. Symptoms vary depending on the gas or vapor inhaled and how long a person is exposed to it.

GENERAL SYMPTOMS

- Rapid breathing—the patient may cough, gasp for breath, and find it difficult to talk

- Skin becomes gray-blue (called cyanosis)—this is especially noticeable at the ears, lips, inside the mouth, and at the fingertips

- Inability to think clearly—as oxygen levels fall, the patient will become increasingly restless and anxious, and possibly aggressive

- The patient may complain of feeling sick and may even vomit

1. **Call emergency services.** Do not enter a room or building if you suspect fumes. Call 911 and ask for the fire department. Tell the dispatcher that there are people in the building.

2. **Help the patient away from the fumes.** If the patient is able to get away from the source of the fumes or the

DANGEROUS FUMES

FUMES	SOURCE	SYMPTOMS
SMOKE	Fires—as fire uses oxygen to burn, smoke contains very low oxygen levels. Smoke may also contain toxic gases given off by other materials as they burn.	Noisy breathing, coughing, hoarseness, black or gray saliva (spit), and fluids in the lungs. Skin color may range from gray-blue to cherry-red. As the condition worsens, the patient may lose consciousness or stop breathing. The heat may burn nose hairs, and there may be burns in the throat and inside the nose.
CARBON MONOXIDE (CO)	Colorless, odorless gas that is a by-product of incomplete burning of any fossil fuel. For example, exhausts, gas fires, faulty gas boilers or water heaters, and paraffin heaters.	Mild symptoms are headache, nausea, vomiting, drowsiness, and poor coordination. In more moderate or severe cases there may be confusion, chest pain, shortness of breath, and/or unconsciousness.
SOLVENTS	Lighter fuels, glues, paints, cleaning fluids, camping gas canisters, and aerosol sprays.	General symptoms of fumes, plus headaches and possible loss of consciousness. Solvent use can cause the heart to stop (cardiac arrest). The patient may also have an obstructed airway as a result of breathing solvents from a plastic bag.
CARBON DIOXIDE (CO_2)	Environmental gas, produced naturally and through human activities. It can accumulate in deep enclosed spaces, such as wells. High concentrations can occur in places that are crowded and have poor ventilation. The gas is normally odorless but can be detected at very high concentrations.	General symptoms of fumes, plus headache, breathlessness, a dramatic increase in breathing and pulse rate, tinnitus, and impaired vision. Eventual unconsciousness.

building, stay outside and help her to safety. Never enter the building yourself.

3. **Treat any injury.** Help the patient to sit down. Assess her injuries and treat any burns (see page 126). She may have inhaled smoke, and there could be burns to the mouth,

throat, and windpipe (airways). Loosen any clothing around the neck and chest to help breathing.

4. **Monitor the patient.** Check and note the level of consciousness, breathing, and pulse. Recheck regularly until medical help arrives. If a patient becomes unconscious, open the airway and check breathing. Be prepared to begin CPR (see page 83).

PRECAUTIONS

- Make sure that everyone in your house knows how to escape if there is a fire. Install smoke detectors on every floor of your home. If they are battery operated, check them every week to ensure that they still work.

- Carbon monoxide (CO) is a colorless, odorless, highly toxic gas. Depending on the concentration, CO gas can render a person unconscious within hours. Carbon monoxide can accumulate if solid fuel appliances, such as gas fires, boilers, or water heaters, are badly maintained or faulty. Appliances should be checked at least annually.

- Install CO detector alarms. Put them in every room where there is a fossil fuel appliance. Choose alarms that give visual and audible warnings when there is a buildup of the gas. If the detector alarms are battery operated, check them once a week to ensure that they are still working.

INSECT BITES

If someone has an extreme allergic reaction to an insect bite, the result can be fatal. Even if the person bitten does not have a severe response, many insects carry diseases—some of them serious—so all bites need to be treated with care.

INSECT BITES

1. **Do not scratch.** Apply calamine lotion, ibuprofen gel, or antihistamine cream to reduce swelling and soothe the itching.

2. **Watch for allergic reactions.** In extreme cases, a condition called anaphylaxis can occur rapidly after a bite (see page 74). Symptoms including wheezing, difficulty in swallowing, and faintness may occur. If you experience any of these reactions, get medical help at once.

TICK BITES

1. **Use tweezers.** Take hold of the tick as close to the skin as possible, and pull gently. Its mouthparts are barbed, but a steady action should pull the tick free.

2. **Store the tick.** If you are in an area where tick-borne diseases are common, keep the tick so that you can have it analyzed if you develop any symptoms. A small screw cap covered with cling wrap or tape makes an ideal impromptu specimen container, or use anything sealable, such as a water bottle. Wash your hands if you touched the tick.

3. **Clean the bite.** Swab the bite with antiseptic, apply antiseptic cream, and cover it. Rarely, an anaphylactic reaction may occur. If after a few days it does not seem to be healing, seek medical advice, as infection is quite common.

PRECAUTIONS

Mosquitoes can carry malaria, yellow fever, dengue fever, and encephalitis. Ticks may pass on Lyme disease, tsetse flies can carry sleeping sickness, and sandflies—found on beaches—may harbor leishmaniasis.

FLYING INSECTS

- Mosquitoes are most active from two hours before dusk right through until dawn. If possible, head indoors just before the sun goes down.

- Use a repellent. The most effective ones contain DEET, up to a maximum concentration of 30 percent for adults and 10 percent for children.

- At night, sleep under mosquito netting or in a room protected by screens. If the screens are open by day, close them and use a mosquito spray to clear the room before you go to bed.

- Treat clothes and mosquito nets with permethrin to repel all types of flying and crawling insects.

CRAWLING INSECTS

- Ticks are active from May to September, so in areas where tick-borne disease is common, avoid prime tick habitats if possible.

- Ticks live in woodland and other well-vegetated areas. They climb up the stems of plants from where they can cling to any passing host. When out walking, wear long-sleeved shirts and long pants, and tuck your pants into your socks or boots. DEET-based repellents also help.

- Check your skin carefully after a walk. Most ticks are harmless, but remove them quickly to reduce the chances of acquiring an infection.

INFECTED WOUND

Infection occurs when disease-causing microorganisms (germs) enter the body and multiply. Any break in the skin allows bacteria to enter the body, increasing the chance of infection. Check daily for signs of infection; any wound that does not start to heal within 48 hours is at risk. Early diagnosis can reduce any danger to the injured person's overall health.

SYMPTOMS OR SIGNS OF INFECTION

- The wound and surrounding skin feels hot

- The area around the injury is swollen

- Yellow pus in the wound and/or redness around the wound— there may be red "trails" leading away from the wound

- Swollen lymph glands in the armpit or groin

- Raised temperature and the patient may feel generally unwell

1. **Remove old dressings.** Take off the old dressings and dispose of them hygienically. Carefully clean around the wound with soap and water or alcohol-free antiseptic wipes.

2. **Cover the wound.** Place a sterile dressing over the infected wound and secure it with a bandage. Raise and support the injury, for example in a sling (see page143) if necessary.

3. **Seek medical advice.** Tell the person to arrange an appointment with his doctor, as a course of antibiotics may be needed, or take him to the hospital.

UNDERSTANDING INFECTION

- **Infection sources.** Germs can enter the body via the cause of injury, for example a dirty knife. Alternatively they can come from a person's clothing, hands, or breath. There may also be tiny particles of dirt or dead tissue in a wound.

- **Wound care.** Good hygiene reduces risk. Wash your hands thoroughly with soap and water before treating a patient. If water is unavailable, use alcohol gel. Wear disposable gloves—ideally nonlatex gloves, as many people are allergic to latex. Bleeding naturally flushes out most, if not all, the dirt, but you should always carefully wash around the wound as well to remove dirt from surrounding skin.

- **Tetanus immunization.** Tetanus is a very serious disease resulting from microorganisms found in soil and manure. It is rare in the United States, as most people are protected against this infection through immunization.

GRAVEL GRAZE

The greatest danger from this type of wound is infection from bacteria in the gravel and soil. Bleeding may be controlled easily with direct pressure and elevation. Medical attention will be needed for a large or small graze where dirt has become embedded in the wound. There is a risk of tetanus infection with any dirty wound.

POINTS TO NOTE WHEN CHECKING THE PATIENT

- The wound may be extensive and/or the bleeding severe.

- The wound may be very dirty. Dirt may be plugging the bleeding, which may start only after all the dirt has been washed off.

- Do not try to remove anything embedded in the wound. Seek medical advice.

- Tell the patient to seek medical advice if a fever develops, the wound fails to heal, swelling or redness develops, or it feels hot, as this may mean that the wound has become infected (see page 184).

THE DANGER OF TETANUS

Tetanus is a potentially fatal bacterial infection that can develop when a particular bacterium (germ) found in soil enters your body via a wound or an animal bite. The risk is greatest if the wound is deep or there is manure in the soil, but even small wounds, such as a prick from a thorn, can cause tetanus.

Tetanus infection is rare in the United States because of vaccinations. If the wound is dirty, seek medical advice if the patient has never been immunized or is unsure how many injections have been given in the past.

1. **Control bleeding.** Apply direct pressure over a sterile wound dressing or clean pad and raise the injury to control the bleeding.

2. **Wash wound.** Once the bleeding stops, remove the pad. Keep the injury raised and rinse the wound under cold running water to wash away any loose dirt. If there is no running water, use alcohol-free antiseptic wipes. Pat it dry.

3. **Clean around wound.** Gently place a fresh sterile dressing over the wound. Carefully wipe dirt from around the injury—you can use clean gauze pads. Use a separate pad for each stroke. Pat the area dry.

4. **Dress wound.** Cover the affected area with a plaster or a sterile wound dressing if the injury is extensive. If it has been thoroughly cleaned, the graze should heal on its own.

5. **Go to the hospital.** All large wounds need medical attention, as does any wound with gravel embedded in it. Carefully cleaned minor injuries should heal naturally. Ask the patient whether she has been immunized against tetanus; if not, she should tell the hospital team or her own doctor.

SUNBURN

Damage (burning) caused by over-exposure to the ultraviolet (UV) rays in sunlight is called sunburn. Two main types of UV rays cause damage to skin: UVB rays are responsible for the majority of sunburn and can lead to skin cancer; UVA rays penetrate deeper into the skin causing aging but contribute much less toward sunburn.

When skin is exposed to sunlight, it produces a pigment called melanin to provide some protection from UV rays. The less melanin in the skin, the less the skin is protected. People with fair skin naturally have lower levels of melanin than those with darker hair or skin. Most sunburn is caused by exposure to bright sunlight, but it can also occur on overcast days, especially at high altitudes, or from sitting under a sun lamp. Overexposure to the sun may also result in heat exhaustion or heatstroke. Seek medical advice for dizziness, headaches, and nausea.

MILD SUNBURN

- Itchy skin, especially in the days after the initial exposure, which eventually peels

- Skin very sore to touch, and may feel "tight" as it begins to heal

SEVERE SUNBURN

- Possible fever

- Blisters

- Swelling

- There may also be symptoms of heat-related illness, such as headaches, dizziness, and nausea

SUN PROTECTION

- **Cover up.** Wear clothes that cover the shoulders (sun-proof clothing is ideal), a hat that protects the neck, and sunglasses.

- **Stay in the shade.** Do this as much as possible, but always when the sun is at its peak—between 11 a.m. and 3 p.m.

- **Always use sunscreen.** Use cream with a sun protection factor (SPF) of at least 15 and reapply it at least every two hours and immediately after swimming. For very pale skin, use SPF 50. Make sure children are well protected, as their skin is more delicate than an adult's.

1. **Move patient to the shade.** Give the patient a towel or light cotton clothing to cover affected areas and help into the shade.

2. **Cool the burned area.** Tell the patient to cool his skin by sponging it with lukewarm water or by having a tepid shower. For a large area of skin, he may want to cool the area by soaking in a cool bath.

3. **Drink water and fluids.** Make sure the patient drinks plenty of fluids to replace the fluid lost through sweating and to cool down. Do not let him drink alcohol because it will dehydrate him further.

4. **Apply creams.** For mild sunburn, tell the patient to apply a moisturizing lotion or aftersun lotion. Aftersun lotions help to cool and moisturize the skin, which helps prevent the "tight" feeling that can develop as the skin heals, but they do not provide protection from the sun. Calamine lotion may also relieve itching and soreness.

TAKE CARE

- Mild sunburn can be treated at home. Advise the person to stay out of the sun, either inside or in the shade, and to keep the area covered with light (preferably cotton) clothing until the skin has healed. The patient's skin may also flake or peel after a few days. This is the body's way of protecting itself: the skin cells have been damaged and are at risk of becoming cancerous, so the body sheds them.

- Adults may take one of their usual painkillers, such as acetaminophen or ibuprofen, to relieve discomfort. A child can be given appropriate doses of children's acetaminophen or children's ibuprofen.

- A patient with severe burns will need to be assessed at a hospital. As with any burn, there is a risk of fluid loss and infection.

- Do not touch blisters caused by sunburn, treat as for burns. Cool the burned area with water until the pain eases. Cover the blister with plastic kitchen wrap or a non-fluffy dressing and take the patient to a hospital.

- Severe sunburn in which the skin has blistered needs hospital treatment. Take the patient to the hospital or call emergency services if the blistering is extensive.

CHECK FOR MOLES

Regularly check your skin for moles. They are formed by a collection of skin pigment cells called melanocytes. Most are normal and harmless, but in a few cases they can develop into malignant melanoma, an aggressive form of skin cancer. If new moles develop or existing moles and/or freckles change, for example grow or start to bleed, consult a doctor to test for skin cancer.

QUICK REFERENCE INDEX

Also Available from Reader's Digest

The most useful information in a most useful format, from the people who have been getting to the heart of the matter for almost 100 years.

The Reader's Digest Quintessential Guides—
The Best Advice, Straight to the Point!

ON SALE NOW

An A to Z of Ingenious Tips for Stretching Your Dollars
- Cut household bills
- Spend less on groceries (and eat better!)
- Find unexpected sales and freebies
- Make the most of your health care
- And much more!

$14.99 • Concealed Spiral • 978-1-62145-248-5

AVAILABLE SOON

The Truth Behind the Foods We Eat and What to Choose for Optimum Health
- The enemies of good nutrition and the food heroes revealed
- Tips on shopping, storing, preparing, and serving
- Scientifically proven evidence of the link between good food, good health, and long life

$14.99 • Concealed Spiral • 978-1-62145-293-5

An A to Z of Lawns, Flowers, Shrubs, Fruits, and Vegetables
- What to grow where
- Design gardens for beauty and productivity
- Deal with plant diseases, pests, and weeds
- Pick the right tools
- And much more!

$14.99 • Concealed Spiral • 978-1-62145-291-1

Reader's
digest